Love and Violence

SUNY series in Contemporary Italian Philosophy
Silvia Benso and Brian Schroeder, editors

Love and Violence

The Vexatious Factors of Civilization

Lea Melandri
translated by Antonio Calcagno

Published by State University of New York Press, Albany

From the Italian original, *Amore e violenza*, Lea Melandri
© 2011 Bollati Boringhieri editore, Torino
English translation © 2019 State University of New York

All rights reserved

Printed in the United States of America

No part of this book may be used or reproduced in any manner whatsoever without written permission. No part of this book may be stored in a retrieval system or transmitted in any form or by any means including electronic, electrostatic, magnetic tape, mechanical, photocopying, recording, or otherwise without the prior permission in writing of the publisher.

For information, contact State University of New York Press, Albany, NY
www.sunypress.edu

Library of Congress Cataloging-in-Publication Data

Names: Melandri, Lea, author.
Title: Love and violence : the vexatious factors of civilization / Lea Melandri ; translation by Antonio Calcagno.
Other titles: Amore e violenza. English
Description: Albany : State University of New York Press, [2018] | Series: SUNY series in contemporary Italian philosophy | Includes bibliographical references.
Identifiers: LCCN 2018006714| ISBN 9781438472652 (hardcover : alk. paper) | ISBN 9781438472669 (e-book)
Subjects: LCSH: Feminism—Italy. | Man-woman relationships. | Women—Violence against. | Violence in men.
Classification: LCC HQ1638 .M443713 2018 | DDC 305.420945—dc23 LC record available at https://lccn.loc.gov/2018006714

10 9 8 7 6 5 4 3 2 1

Contents

Acknowledgments   vii

Translator's Introduction   ix

Preface   xi

LOVE AND VIOLENCE

1   The Body and the Polis   3

2   Loving Mothers   37

3   The Circle of Men   73

4   The Disquieting Slumber of the West   95

5   The Unstoppable Revolution   111

Notes   137

Index   145

Acknowledgments

THIS TRANSLATION would not have been possible without the generosity of Dean Sauro Camiletti of King's University College, Canada, who, along with the College's Research Grants Committee, awarded me a grant that enabled me to finish the project. I am greatly indebted to Kathy Daymond, the English-language editor of this volume. I would like to thank my research assistant, William Cockrell, who patiently looked up and checked references and quotations. He also read the final draft of the text to check for any potential errors. Paola Melchiori diligently read the English translation to make sure that I captured the Italian sense of Lea Melandri's ideas and insights. I owe a debt of gratitude to Silvia Benso and Brian Schroeder, the editors of the SUNY series in Contemporary Italian Philosophy. Finally, I would like to thank Andrew Kenyon and the staff of SUNY Press for their support and work on this translation.

— Antonio Calcagno
King's University College, Canada

Translator's Introduction

LEA MELANDRI represents a stream of Italian feminist thought that occupies a unique place in the history of philosophy. In contradistinction to Anglo-American feminism, which emphasized both equality and emancipation as ends, Italian feminism can be said to have stressed female difference, autonomy, and liberation. The discussion of difference was also taken up by French feminist philosophers, including Hélène Cixous, Luce Irigaray, Monique Wittig, and Julia Kristeva. But what marks Italian feminist thought as unique is the desire to integrate both practice and theory. Lea Melandri's writings express and always return to the need for integrating both theory and praxis.

Deeply influenced by psychoanalytic theory and practice, Melandri's *Love and Violence* argues two central claims. First, love and violence ought to be viewed as coexistent. Society sees love and violence as unrelated opposites, ultimately refusing to see how often they coincide. This has severe implications for the lives of women, for the violence they bear at the hands of their male counterparts is either ignored or even justified because of the unconscious, societal privileging of love over violence. Love and loving are supposed to mitigate or nullify the violence and suffering that women endure, either because women (as wives and mothers) are expected to love, forgive and/or accept aggression, or because it is part of the natural order of society.

Second, if it is true that love and violence often coincide, as Freud rightly shows in his discussion of eros and thanatos, especially at the level of the unconscious, then how does this psychic structure play out in male-female relationships? It is Lea Melandri's response to this question that distinguishes her philosophy from other feminist thinkers. She argues that the unconscious bifurcation of male and female includes the dynamic of love and violence insofar as male aggression forcibly structures the female and society to accept horrendous forms of violence against women, and all in the name of love. Melandri closely examines motherhood, the workplace, public life, male-female love relationships, and even social phenomena to demonstrate how the unconscious bifurcation of male and female deeply instills and justifies the need for violence against women and how love ultimately can be used to cover over the brutality and suffering caused by such violence. The practice of the unconscious or consciousness-raising is one way in which one can begin to uncover and see both the unconscious dynamics and the playing out of love and violence in daily life. Seeing how this complex dynamic plays out demands that we change our conscious practices: we must reject its deep roots and create for women a public space in which they can autonomously and fully express their unique differences. Conscious practices aimed at ending violence against women will undo, or at least have the potential to undo, the unconscious writing of a more traditional primary scene in which women are subject to and forced to accept male violence and aggression.

Italian feminism and feminist thought of the 1970s were marked by an explosion of theory and practices that had a wide-ranging impact on art, politics, literature, social thinking, psychology, and philosophy. Lea Melandri's ideas were and are deeply influential. She continues to travel throughout Italy and Europe to present her philosophy. It is my hope that, with this translation, readers will become familiar with one of Italy's more original philosophers, who tries to integrate both thinking and living, philosophy and doing.

— Antonio Calcagno
King's University College, Canada

Preface

WE MUST NOT BE MISLED by the assault on women's dignity by the degrading images that represent them on television and in advertising and the various pleas to women to rebel against them. The female body has occupied media space for many years, but the pornographic imaginary now contaminates the order of discourse and language. Exhibitionism and voyeurism, deliberately wedded together on reality television, have permeated the passive enjoyment, if such enjoyment can be said to have ever existed, of the viewer. The sudden reawakening of offended moral conscience, of feminine intelligence "humiliated" by the commercialization of its sex, comes after a series of events that could not have left us indifferent, for the protagonist of these events was one of the highest officers of the state, namely, the prime minister of the Republic of Italy. These events involved the casual exchange of sexual favors for money, political careers, and even television roles.

Television viewers see a continuous flow of women-objects, women-images, and women-ornaments. We see this flow of women on daytime, prime-time, and late-night television; we see it on programs about culture and in lightweight entertainment, on both publicly supported and private channels. The female body, as aesthetic embellishment or erotic stimulus, as something that simply stands next to the words of men, no matter their political orientation, is recognized as the signifier of origins—a signifier unequivocally deployed by the dominant sex. Furthermore, the *evidence* about women's sexual objectification and their value as sexual objects to be exchanged, which lies before all eyes, on the streets and on the walls in subway stations, on television and in the newspapers, needs no scandalous dramatization in order to be made *visible*. Even so, Silvio Berlusconi, Italy's prime minister, and a plethora of showgirls and escorts were implicated in a series of events that corroborated this evidence. Those engaged in feminist culture and practice find talk about the "silence of women" irritating, but we must have the courage to ask ourselves uncomfortable and embarrassing questions about what appears as a glaring contradiction: a movement that has given to women previously unknown mobility and world citizenship nevertheless finds women to be "adaptable" and disinclined to initiate conflict. Agile acrobats, women sustain the impossible reconciliation of separate realities: the home and the polis, the body and thought, feminine fragility and virile endurance, personal feelings and the requirements of social relations.

Public space, which has as its founding act the exclusion of women, has, in recent decades, become more feminized. At the same time, however, precisely where one might have expected conflict between the sexes to intensify—that is, in the traditional preserves of male knowledge and power, such as the economy, politics, science, and so on—such conflict seems to have diminished. The predominance of the female presence in historically traditional loci—for example, schools and social services—is guaranteed by the notion of woman, conceived either as a "natural presence" or a "divine mission," as "the eternal mother, even when she is a virgin" (Paolo Mantegazza), devoted to the care of others, even beyond the confines of the home. But feminization, reaching into the deepest folds of the social fabric, has achieved more; it is exalted as a source of innovation and as the precious resource of an economic, political, and cultural system that is feeling the effects of the decline of the ancient divide between the private and public spheres, between nature and culture, sexuality and politics—the very demarcations that have until now permitted the historical community of men to think themselves the inheritors of a superior type of humanity.

In those newspapers allied with Confindustria,[1] including, for example, *Il Sole 24 Ore* (The 24-hour Sun), a day does not pass without praise for the "W value"—the particular value of women, namely, a relational and nurturing quality that women allegedly bring to the highest levels of management and to an always more flexible and immaterial system of production. In the professions and in work relations generally, the example of the "supermom," capable of excelling at both child care and career, is heralded. But the "feminine" has truly exploded in the field of communication—in television, show business, and advertising, in particular—taking by surprise those who foresaw women achieving, always slowly and with great effort, a new autonomy, even if that autonomy was modeled on the conventional male form.

The intense debate about the connection between large numbers of beautiful showgirls and other female performers and powerful men—men so powerful that, unchallenged, they were able to mount beauty pageants in the Italian Lower House of Parliament—has produced cries of "barbarism" from feminists and the fear of the failure of a century of female emancipation. But even here our judgments are only approximate; they are far from the analysis carried out by women on what *remains* of gender stereotypes despite evident changes in the social context. Liberty and hard-won rights do not seem to have radically undermined the most captivating aspect of sexual roles, that is, complementarity—the "profound but irrational instinct," as Virginia Woolf wrote, that favors the theory that only the union of men and women, of the masculine and the feminine, can "produce the greatest satisfaction," can render the mind "fecund and creative."

In this ideal conjoining of diverse natures, the love of couples, as well as its originary antecedent, the mother-son relation, are nourished. Understudied or ignored, these most intimate zones of the relation between the sexes reappear today under the guise of an emancipation that we must recognize as deformed.

Feminists, rather than advocating that women simply mimic or conform to traditional male attributes, challenged the traditional female attributes themselves—that is, maternity and, as Rousseau put it, the "attracting power" of women. In response to this challenge and redefinition of women's sexuality and power, men came to regard these female attributes, and feminism itself, as the tools of an appropriation of power, as mechanisms of social climbing, as *payback*.

But if our so-called emancipation is now considered to belong to a discredited feminism, today it is the feminine—the body, sexuality, the maternal attitude—that liberates us as such and occupies in the public sphere a place that seeks to be an indispensable complement to male culture.

Patriarchy is devouring itself, and the scaffolding upon which the polis is built is creaking. This tenuous condition of the polis offers women, who are included-excluded, the chance to unveil the essential power of what has always been their private strength.

The feminization of the public sphere softens the conflict between the sexes, and, as in the illusion of love, the possibility of a "truce" flickers. But, precisely like the delusion of love, in which the notion of the complementarity between the sexes serves to obscure the power of men over women, feminization, merely by introducing complementarity into the public sphere, does not constitute, as Pierre Bourdieu noted, a "supreme form" of female power, "because [the notion of complementarity that underlies the lauding of feminization] is the most subtle, the most invisible form" of men's power over women.[2]

It is necessary, therefore, to probe the end point of the voyage undertaken by Freud—the "adventurer of the soul" and great investigator of happiness—namely, the "bedrock" of his "rejection of the feminine," the inexplicable interweaving of eros and thanatos, the hate that inevitably arises from love, in personal life and in the public sphere.

The writings in this book, like all of my earlier publications, were born from the fortuitous encounter between personal research and collective reflection, a precious good that today has largely fallen into disuse. Nevertheless, the practice of collective reflection persists, waiting for better times, in the constellation of the thousands of other-than-"silent" groups in Italy and elsewhere that helped to reawaken feminine consciousness in the 1970s.

LOVE AND VIOLENCE

A friend is the place where one can calmly deposit oneself.
This is not often the case with those you hold dear.
—Rossana Rossanda, *La perdita*

To Rossana Rossanda and our beautiful friendship

CHAPTER ONE

THE BODY AND THE POLIS

THE NON-PRESENTABLE CITIZENSHIP OF THE BODY

The reduction of the thinking body to a mere organism in a biological view of life is the way in which the human being has come to terms with its animal root and, hence, its mortality, as well as with a perturbing origin made possible by the exclusion of human beings' biological nature from history. The idea of a hidden beginning or foundation, destined to remain out of sight, is the imaginary effect of an abstract division, which has sadly become the materiality of relations, powers, cultural constructs, habits, and common sense. Certain enigmas, which call into question the contradictions between civilized life and human drives, and which revolve around the originary schism between love and death, hope and nihilism, remain unexplored. Coupled with the "enigma of dualism," to borrow an expression from Otto Weininger,[1] one finds the "enigma of sex"—the rejection of the feminine, the "bedrock" upon which Freud's psychoanalytic voyage was based—and the "enigma of history"—the delivery of oneself as a "thing," as "merchandise," into the hands of another, which Marx, in his *Economic and Philosophic Manuscripts of 1844*, identified as the result of economic alienation.

"Man," writes Giorgio Agamben, "is a living being who, in language, separates from and opposes to itself its own bare life. The human being continues to be in relation with bare life in an inclusive exclusion.... In western politics, bare life has a unique privilege: it is that upon which exclusion founds the city of human beings."[2] The original schism, for Agamben, opposes thought to the body, transforming the inextricable concrete singularity of every being into a relation between sovereign power and a life bereft of humanity, between an idea and a thing. In Agamben's lucid analysis of the birth of the polis (that is, how the abstract figure of the biological body is produced and deployed), we are struck by the fact that he did not see the vehement conviction with which the man-son believes himself to be different from the body that delivered him into the world—a body identified with a "lower" nature, with animality, and, consequently, a body understood as the very depository of its own material heritage is imbricated with and mistaken for the process of socialization.

"But it is in darkness, and as darkness itself, that the body was *conceived*. The body was conceived and shaped in Plato's cave and as a cave, it is the prison or tomb of the soul."[3] From this prison or tomb, the anguish of suffering connected with all that is directly linked to bodily experience is born, including sexuality, old age, sickness, and death. The obsessive use of the body as meaning, metaphor, or discourse also arises here, as does the reduction of the body to a machine or a scientific phenomenon.

The endless aggression and exploitation exerted by the historical community of human beings on the world's natural resources can be viewed as an evident but insufficiently explored analogy with forms of the male domination of the body from which one receives life, and with which one is completely unified at the origin of life. Politics and economy bear distinguishing signs. In *Civilization and Its Discontents*, written in 1929, Freud observed:

> The communists believe they have found the path to deliverance from our evils. According to them, man is wholly good and is well-disposed to his neighbor; but the institution of private property has corrupted his nature. The ownership of private wealth gives the individual power, and with it the temptation to ill-treat his neighbor, while the man who is excluded from possession is bound to rebel in hostility against his oppressor. If private property were abolished, all wealth held in common, and everyone allowed to share in the enjoyment of

it, ill-will and hostility would disappear among men. Since everyone's needs would be satisfied, no one would have any reason to regard another as his enemy; all would willingly undertake the work that was necessary. I have no concern with any economic criticisms of the communist system; I cannot inquire into whether the abolition of private property is expedient or advantageous. But I am able to recognize that the psychological premises on which the system is based are an untenable illusion. In abolishing private property, we deprive the human love of aggression of one of its instruments, certainly a strong one, though certainly not the strongest; but we have in no way altered the differences in power and influence which are misused by aggressiveness, nor have we altered anything in its nature. Aggressiveness was not created by property. It reigned almost before property had given up its primal, anal form; it forms the basis of every relation of affection and love among people (with the single exception, perhaps, of the mother's relation to her male child).[4]

The power of love and the coercion of work—the progenitors of human civilization—are more similar and intertwined than we tend to think. The same thing can be said of the tragic connection between love and hate, in personal relationships as well as in relations between groups, peoples, and cultures. The destruction of war is viewed as necessary in order to save what we love. Separating the idea of the biological body from human activity, from all the manifestations of physical acts and psychic energy, human beings have created a presupposition for every form of alienation: a condition of being in which the human being becomes "other than itself" and comes to regard itself as a foreign and hostile external power; the human being becomes property, a thing that can be subjugated, controlled, and manipulated by others. In his 1844 manuscripts, Marx argued:

> Political economy starts with the fact of private property. It does not explain it.... Political economy throws no light on the cause of the division between labor and capital.... The *devaluation* of the world

> of men is in direct proportion to the *increasing value* of the world of things. Labor produces not only commodities; it produces itself and the worker as a *commodity*—and this at the same rate at which it produces commodities in general....
>
> ... The worker puts his life into the object; but now it no longer belongs to him but to the object.... Therefore, the greater this product, the less is he himself. The *alienation* of the worker in his product means not only that his labor becomes an object, an *external* existence, but that it exists *outside him*, independently, as something alien to him, and that it becomes a power on its own confronting him. It means that the life which he has conferred on the object confronts him as something hostile and alien....
>
> ... It is *forced labor*.[5]

How can we not see that "forced labor," destructive and hateful, has been imposed on women as their destiny, demanding the sacrifice of their sexuality and their very being? Has this same destiny been imposed upon the sex that has framed itself as the protagonist of history? What can the "giving of oneself" (which is called for by patriarchal, secular, and religious ideology) be if not confirmation of the originary alienation of feminine being, reduced to a reproductive function or to the status of merchandise for exchange? Is the marriage-based family, which the Italian constitution defines as a "natural society," not the locus of such an abstraction? By opposing male and female roles, has the family not rendered natural functions such as eating, drinking, procreating, clothing, and nurturing ourselves as our final and civilized ends?

> Thought that removes the body is thought that renounces love, and with it the most important questions about suffering, death, and happiness.
>
> It has been written: "Old age is not the extreme limit of the human condition; rather, it is the human condition in its most authentic state." ... I would add a question to this affirmation:

"This life, which is only life, nothing but the life that belongs to the old person as the human condition, has it the right to asylum in our world? What else is it but an entanglement of powers that cross through life itself, which often render life itself wholly insignificant?"[6]

But as Nancy observes,

But where are bodies? Bodies are primarily at work, ... suffering at work. Bodies are primarily traveling toward work, returning to work, awaiting rest; bodies quickly take rest and then leave it behind; they stay at work. They also are working, incorporating themselves into commodities; they themselves become commodities. Bodies are forced labor ... channeled by their own monetized force, moving toward that surplus capital that collects and concentrates *in them*.[7]

No culture other than western culture has succeeded so well at "inventing the body as bare," thereby simultaneously establishing the premise for the artificial renaming and regeneration of the body, for a reconfigured body that now catastrophically aims to replace the bare body. "We have not laid the body bare," says Jean-Luc Nancy; rather, "we have invented it, and the body is nudity, and there is no nudity other than its own, and this nudity is the *most foreign* of all foreign bodies."[8]

From the original cave, in which the dream of eros, which is locked in the eternal immobility of a prehistoric desire to become more than oneself (for example, in a romantic couple, in a closed group based on identity, ethnicity, the nation, etc.), is unpresentable or inexpressible, the body generally emerges as an unheard-of protagonist that has returned in order to take its revenge. Given that the body erupted onto the public stage as the effect of the dissolution of the border between home and city, individual and society, nature and artifice, it could do nothing but reconsider the phenomenology in which it had been constituted, folded one way or another into the "reign of the mind" that both exalted and subjected it, rendering it simultaneously insignificant and useful for bestowing sense to the collectivity. The word "body," in its metaphorical usage, suggests that the body was able to enter the polis as a citizen at the same time that real bodies were rejected from the city.

In the contemporary global scene, which is controlled by forceful powers that include the state, the church, the market, science, and technology—all of which have been revealed to be biopolitical powers—we find not only the "fabulous" bodies of technology that have transformed the human being into a kind of "prosthetic God," but also the people of the world, many of whom have been reduced to a "wound . . . bodies of misery, of famine; beaten bodies, infected and bloated bodies, and overly fed bodies." We find the "damned of the earth," and their damnation touches us all when we lose power over that which surrounds us and over our own bodies. Thus damned, we "become like an abandoned house left to the care of others." The relentlessness of getting our bodies in shape and the protection and extension of biological survival at any cost are but the other face of the human being's ultimate and ineluctable anguish, born from its dependency upon a body that is not its own—a body that signifies the human being's mortal destiny, its fall from grace and its need for salvation.

Since the beginning of the 1970s, Elvio Fachinelli has observed "a breakdown of the civic superego" as a result of "sexual and aggressive drives that were previously removed or sublimated: . . . on one hand, sexual permissiveness and, on the other hand, the reappropriation of aggression on the part of single individuals or groups."[9] Facing the dangers of desiccation or sterility, eros deployed a historical trick, a new barbarism, in order to secure its continuance. Newly formed constituencies during those years of estrangement looked upon a story that, even in its ideal goals of social justice, equality, and a "communism" of goods, continued to privilege the means of production, which only served to annihilate the individual in her or his irreducible complexity and confine him or her within the limits of social conditioning: these were the students of 1968, the "plural subjects" of nonauthoritarian movements, and the feminists.

As the dissident desire of the students of 1968 was rapidly eclipsed, as their place was ceded to the "pure revolutionaries" such as those in

Marxist-Leninist parties, who then reproduced the same conditions as those cultivated by the apparatus of domination (dependency, passivity, the delegation of tasks), it fell to the theory and practice of the women's movement to establish a process that was responsive to the crisis at the same time as it was able to undertake the redefinition of a politics—long fettered by patriarchy, the original alienation—increasingly subject to economization.

To narrate and write not *about* the body, but *the* body, as Nancy urges us to do, to launch a politics not only based *on* life, but *of* life, meant, for feminism, positioning personal stories as central. Feminists posited the thinking body as paramount. The thinking body—a body affected by the passions, a body that renders all human beings similar—reconfigures the female body, so long regarded as a "black hole," as the sediment of a memory and culture yet to be explored, the precious archive of an "unpresentable" history from which we have for too long averted our eyes.

> The West has constructed a mode of rational engagement, an unembodied thought, in which reason turns to reason. Feminism was the first movement of liberation to break with this sacred aspiration.... The problem of the task can be summarized in the following demand: the return to the body.... The path of emancipation passes here today: let us seize this fundamental experience, the contingent body.[10]

The predominant public discourse about what are inappropriately called "ethical questions," which the media refer to as "real-life questions," recast and foregrounded the body and its vicissitudes while, at the same time, confining it to the private sphere—a sphere that precludes collective reflection, which, in an earlier era, was known as consciousness-raising. A culture capable of rethinking the age-old enmity between life and politics, which could bring to light the enduring connections between society and the individual, between the ever-changing time of history and the "invariability" of interiority, no longer exists: here, one runs the risk of being wedged in by antipolitical attitudes, psychological misery, and the conformism of the masses, which are primarily worried about their peaceful existence. But even more dangerous is the aggressive return of fundamentalist religion, which seeks to restore the privileged place of religion in the social and political fabric of a modernity that seems to have abandoned it.

The Ambiguous Border between Ethics and Politics

Many interpretations of the recent religious revival that threatens what had seemed to be the West's consolidated process of secularization have been put forth, but they all agree that religion offers few certainties. The current religious revival of an archaic, fundamentalist Islam can be seen as analogous to various Roman Catholic campaigns for the revival of a religious culture in the recent past. Pope Benedict XVI lacked neither the violence of his ancient predecessors, now presented as Christian strength, nor their conviction, with which he continues to bind himself to his faithful followers. Confrontation, fear, and envy, which seem to motivate the antiabortion campaign, are legitimized by the cross and militate against the all-too-limited freedom of western women.

For others, clinging to the traditional values of religion espoused by charismatic leaders seemed to offer refuge from the dis-ease of a civilization that had lost its optimism in relation to its own technological, scientific ends. If, at the beginning of the twentieth century, the great "god-prosthesis," with all of its accessory organs, appeared to Freud as less happy than one might have imagined, today, our technological omnipotence is no longer able to eclipse the shadow of death that lingers behind it, even as its reach extends to experimentation on living matter, even as it continues its abuse of the environment and ruthless exploitation of natural resources, and even as it reconfigures relations between classes and peoples of the world. From extensive economic horror, from widespread feelings of insecurity, from the increasing loss of identity, comes the rebirth of a need for a spirituality that enthusiastically revives ancient rites and splendors in the form of New Age religion's simplistic ways.

But there is another aspect of our current situation that deserves our attention, even though it has links to this religious revival—namely, the current political crisis that fails to recognize the separation between the quotidian and the real person, a separation inscribed in the founding act of politics: the expulsion of women from the public sphere, the scission between body and language, home and city, biology and history. Today, the fundamental questions of life that have arisen out of a centuries-long exile emerge in unforeseen places. The object of control, manipulation, and other interventions by the powers of the state, the church, the markets, the courts, science, and the media, these questions also suggest the possibility of cultural and political change. A biologically determined vision of life and the conception of the family as sacred, the concepts of the female body, the couple, birth and death, and the idea of a "divine order," indisputably presupposed by morality, science, and law, all are deteriorating together. The consideration of all these aspects in relation to one another constitutes the freedom with which individuals believe they are able to make decisions about their own lives.

Confronted by this state of affairs, the political Left faces the greater difficulty, while the Right operates with an indifferent lack of scruples on historically familiar terrain that features antipolitical attitudes, populism, the rhetoric of traditional values, the manipulation of affect and of the collective imagination, all of which receive much attention from the contemporary media. As Agamben explained in an interview with the newspaper *Manifesto*, "life devours politics":

> Democracy has become synonymous with the rational management of human beings and things (*oikonomia*): wars become police operations, the popular will turns into public opinion polls, and political choices become a question of management—a management that privileges the home and business, not the city. The space of the political is disappearing.[11]

Although the revenge of the body and all that was confined to the private sphere seems to be affirmed in the apparent "feminization" of work and politics, the body and the feminine have not, in fact, escaped their servitude to the "sovereign power" that seeks to reduce them to the biological, to domestic functions, and servile and complementary attitudes. Conservative political forces, which share a broad and popular consensus around this construct of femininity, risk denying the very "power of life" that has stamped human history from its beginnings. The inadequacy of the Left, which has given rise to the impression of a great void opening before our very eyes, lies in its theoretical and ideological foundations in the Enlightenment: historical materialism, reason, and materiality are directed almost exclusively to matters of rights and the relations of production—matters that cannot address the root of the human, cannot give voice, through political engagement, to what Marx identified as the "passion of the human being," the human need to self-actualize. Though no one any longer speaks of a "superstructure" that arises out of the economic base, the essential questions of life have become marginal, no more than generic and instrumental formulations. The inevitable void produced by a lack of analysis and the evisceration of political culture renders the latter ripe for occupation by forces such as the church and the fundamentalist right, now allies, who claim these matters as their prerogative.

The liberal, secular, and democratic left has, until now, met the Vatican's invasion of the political domain with head-on confrontation, insisting on the opposition between church and state, between public ethics and religious morality—a voluntaristic and unproductive approach that has produced few, if any, results. It would be more useful to analyze the historical links between the two spheres of power, connections that, gaining strength today, are producing hybrid figures such as "faithful atheists." Above all, we must ask how the idea of the secular has changed, how the borders between religion and politics, between ethics and politics, have changed at a time when neither sphere can be regarded as neutral from the perspective of sex. In other words, in addition to what distinguishes and sets these spheres in opposition to one another, we must examine what they hold in common: the history of male domination. The religious sphere aims at the private domain, toward personal life, while the political sphere aims at the public domain. But their complementarity reveals their shared parentage, the matrix in which the unique protagonist of history—the male sex—divides, opposes, and hierarchizes aspects of the human being that are, in fact, inseparable: the biological body and the capacity for thought, economic survival and emotional survival, necessity and freedom.

The new awareness that arose during the women's movement in the 1970s, in which the relation between the sexes was examined through the lenses of the body, sexuality, and personal experience, modified both the border between religion and the secular, and, by demonstrating how morality served to obscure political relations of power, the more ambiguous relation between ethics and politics. The symmetry between the terms "religion" and "the secular" becomes clearer in the context of left-wing debates that declared the urgent need to construct a "public ethics." No one doubts that the Left in Italy has historically lacked values and moral principles; many have written and spoken about the need to fill this vacuum, especially in the context of the discussion of "ethically sensitive questions" such as abortion, artificial insemination, euthanasia, and stem cell research. Given the Left's failings, it was clear that the Left could not mount an effective challenge to the rise of Catholic fundamentalism.

The definition of a "secular ethics," like that of religious ethics, came about through dialogue between secular and religious representatives and aimed to achieve a balance between the secular and religious. This meant that, despite the diversity of forms of ethics, agreement about the meaning of bodily human experience was assumed, and was assumed to refer back to morality, as if human experience were simply a matter of individual conscience. Facts were obfuscated, including the fact that the "questions of life" raise, in a more or less direct way, the relation of power between the sexes as well as the fact that the questions themselves lie squarely at the heart of politics. All of this clearly exposed the crisis of politics and the need for its redefinition. These questions can either portend the abandonment of power—of markets, religion, science, and media—to antipolitical sentiments, or they can serve to launch a process of renewal.

For all these reasons, and in order to resolve any ambiguity as well as to admit the Left's indefensibility, it is important to speak of a "political culture" rather than a "public ethics." The contributions of nonauthoritarian movements and the feminism of the 1970s to the "denaturalization" and "desacralization" of experiences such as birth and death, the relationships of couples, the roles of men and women cannot be forgotten. Together with other "unexpected subjects," the appearance of young people and women on the public stage signaled the discontinuity with history, including that of the socialist revolution. Categories considered until then as "unpolitical"—desire, self-consciousness, the appropriation of one's own body, and recognition of the unconscious—permeated public discourse. Words that had long been paramount in the Left's political lexicon—democracy, liberty, equality—were revisited and reformulated. The abstract figure of the citizen or class was replaced by the whole individual; the thinking body of each sex, embedded in family and social relations, came to the fore.

In the radio conversations between Rossana Rossanda and feminists,[12] the meaning of the word "liberty," for example, changed when the discussion expanded to include the many "non-liberties" that we embody and carry within ourselves. For women, long considered to be neither moral nor spiritual subjects, "liberty" must be, above all, "the freedom to be." There can be no freedom for those who are profoundly alienated from existence. Even the idea of a "party"—its formal framework, hierarchies, bureaucracies, rituals, and myths—substantially changes at the moment the importance of personal relations, of the modification of oneself, comes into view. This modification of the self must be understood as the presupposition for the modification of the world.

The whole of life, and not only labor, viewed from the perspective of the sexes, was thus inserted into the middle of politics, although the insertion of greater numbers of women into the labor force had certainly changed the definition of work. As Pietro Ingrao remarked to Rossanda:

> To face the question of women's liberation is to confront the deep organizational structure of society in general. Let me give an example: If you really wish to deal with the problem of women and work, one must take into account the various dimensions of human development, the occupations themselves, the quality and organization of

labor in work itself. At the same time—this is where things become different—one must deal with the forms of reproduction of society, the ways we conceive of sexuality, couple relationships, the relationships between parents and children, the relation between past and present, the forms and nature of social assistance. This is a historical conception, a secular conception of the private—this is all the conception of the state, the relation between the state and the private.[13]

Following Roberto Esposito's definition of biopolitics[14] as the "immunization" of life and society against pathogenic factors—an immunization that runs the risk of destroying life and society as a result of excessive defense—we maintain that nonauthoritarian movements have represented, on the contrary, an "affirmative biopolitics" capable of producing an undetermined subjectivity and a politics not only *based on* life but *of* life.

In a document written in opposition to the courses offered at the University of Milan in the fall of 1968, the group behind the self-managing children's daycare center, Porta Ticinese, affirmed:

> It is necessary to bring back into the political struggle the relations with the body, with the biological dimension of individuals, even if it contrasts with the long ascetic tradition of the revolutionary movement.... In capitalist society, the biological aspects and realities of human beings—sexual life, labor, birth, the education and nurturing of children—all of these things are frustrated realities, all of them are subject to the radical negation of their value.[15]

Consigning the "questions of life" to the margins of politics, the Left, which believes itself to be "radical," seems incapable of distancing itself from capitalism's prioritization of the economic dimension; it seems to accept the notion that the life of a human being is reducible to production, it behaves as if the crucial moments of life—love, maternity, birth, aging, death—are not subject to institutional pressures, whether those of repressive control or those producing dehumanizing experiences that are no less severe than those caused by the exploitation of labor.

In order to create a political culture that considers the whole of life, one's own body needs to be "put into play"; we need to interrogate our own experience, to see subjectivity as belonging to a thinking body that is sexed, plural, capable of being recognized in its singularity while simultaneously recognizing what it shares in common with others. It is only by advancing into deeper levels of awareness of our own selves that we become capable of accessing a broader horizon. We have to abandon the disastrous dichotomies between particular and universal, between necessity and liberty, dependency and autonomy, individual and collective—often seen as the complementary poles of a relation—that threaten to lead us to the antipolitical positions we see today.

The Body and the Law

What sense does it make to speak of the body in terms of "property," to say "we *have* a body" or that one must "appropriate one's body" when, in reality, *we are bodies*, we are *thinking bodies*? What changes at the moment one becomes conscious that the body is not neutral, but sexed? What changes if we recognize that it is upon both the masculine and the feminine that history, which presents itself as the history of a community of men alone, has constructed the most enduring relations of power: the roles of the sexes, the exclusion of women from the polis, the identification of woman with the nonthinking body, with nature? Above all, what changes when the attention accorded to the body shifts from the public sphere, in which it is seen as an object of rights, laws, ethics, religion, to the private, a zone traditionally considered as nonpolitical? What changes when the body is considered in terms of the particular lived experience of each individual?

When feminism spoke of the "body politic," it was not referring to laws or ethical questions, even though battles of these kinds took place (around, for example, divorce, abortion, and family rights); rather, it sought to bring the whole person, including sex, affective life, and family ties into history, culture, and politics, where they have, in fact, always been, despite their invisibility there. At the same time that feminism constituted a radical rethinking of politics, it served as a symptom of the crisis of politics—politics understood as separate from life, itself mutilated by the disavowal of an essential part of the human, even when it claimed revolution or the creation of an alternative society as its aim. This crisis continues today, but rather than founding a politics of life that reinvented public space, as many of us hoped, feminism has now become antipolitical.

When we speak of the body in terms of "property," "rights," and "public ethics," we risk effacing one term with another. Let us look, for example, at the word "property." How has the objectivation of the term to refer to the person as an owner of his or her body shaped the original split between body and language, between male and female? In *La perdita*, Rossana Rossanda, in conversation with Manuela Fraire, remarked:

> We know that "we are" our bodies, but we think that we "possess" them, as if consciousness has another order of existence, as if we are laid out in a house like a snail in its shell. To say "The body is the first thing that I have" and "this body is me" are not the same thing. Being and having are not identical.[16]

Of all of the irreconcilable oppositions, the most resistant to our pacifying efforts is surely that of an I that is constrained to recognize itself as a stranger in its own body, an I that must exclude the biological cycle from its understanding of itself and that, at the same time, is accorded a "special nature" that is reducible to the material from which other living beings are made. If we accept the split between an I, which imagines itself as eternal and omnipotent, and the material from which it is made (identified with the female body, itself deprived of an I), then the alienation of women is even deeper than one might expect. In *Le altre*, Rossanda emphatically reminds us of the change in the idea of history that was brought about by female consciousness:

> Liberty for her, therefore, is first to find an identity, to be. This is not simply a theme to be investigated, nor has it been resolved by the legal disputes of our democracies: the question of the inalienability of the

person.... For women, this question is as large as the very negation to which they have been subjected; it is immense. Women know that the person remains violated beyond the declarations of law: by misery, orders, ideology, by those projections of the oppression that continue to constrain us from within. This is the deep sense of alienation of the I, which expresses itself in the need to ask oneself: "Who am I?" One also continues to hear the question in feminist slogans such as "I am my own."... This is the most decisive message that the women's movement has given us.[17]

The reappropriation of the body in all of its dimensions, including its biological, psychological, and intellectual aspects, meant, for feminists of the 1970s, beginning from one's personal story, from lived experience, from one's *narrative account of oneself*, in order to explore what had been subordinated by male domination, what had been suppressed in men's vision of the world. By internalizing a male model of the world, women disregarded their own feelings. The critique of institutions of public life was also required, for they, too, by obscuring the body, constructed knowledge and power. As the women of the Center for the Health of Women, founded at Padova in 1974, noted:

> Our struggle is not with Medicine, but with the State, which, through medicine and the health-care system, will continue to expropriate our bodies from us—a body that has been transformed into an instrument of domestic labor, of material reproduction, that is, a body that provides physical, affective, and sexual work for the husband. We are biological and affective reproducers of children.[18]

As self-managing consultants, women sought to reappropriate the body, medicine, and the right to health, and to expand the possibility of living out their experiences within public structures. Consciousness-raising, self-help, self-examination, all of these were radical attempts to reposition the self in terms of one's own physical, psychic, and intellectual being by means of a practice set within *relations among women*—relations dismissed and excluded by institutional forms of knowledge. In this way, women sought to reclaim from the doctor, the psychoanalyst, and the expert knowledge of themselves and the power to change and direct their own lives.

The questions of law, rights, and organized politics, with all of their contradictions, were foregrounded by the problem of abortion. In a meeting of the Circolo De Amicis at Milan in February 1975, a number of voices were raised against positioning the abortion issue as a battle for rights, and various other political organizations echoed this resistance.

> The question of abortion came to the fore for reasons, in part, that were not clear. In a sort of traditional politics, espoused by people whose courage I do not doubt, a logic unfolded in which we became involved. This was done by force and because it involved us in the first person. Everyone wanted us to become involved; priests, ... various parties, opinion groups, the extra-parliamentary left. This could have been viewed as dangerous because it gave us a sense of importance and euphoria, but the fact remains that this push to be involved was imposed upon us from the outside, from above our heads. In my view, we had to find ourselves means with which to confront the question of abortion in nontraditional, political ways. We had to draw upon our own experiences, including positions that may not have been perfectly coherent, but nevertheless we reflected on our own thinking and desire.... It was not in our interest to treat the problem of abortion in itself. Our effort was to link, it seems to me, the problem to our condition and to a particular question, which was that of our sexuality and our body.[19]

Demonstrating just how far removed the analysis of abortion was from the discussion of law and rights was the fact that the principal themes of the meeting were sexuality, frigidity, homosexuality, relations with the mother, vaginal and clitoral sexuality. As the voice for abortion, *Lessico politico delle donne: Donne e medicine* [Women's Political Lexicon: Women and Medicine] summarized the divergent and contested attitudes of women on abortion:

> Whereas secularized persons and Catholics continued to battle against abortion at the parliamentary level, the women's movement continued to debate the issue. Roughly sketching the content of the debate, two central positions can be delineated. One view held that the formalization of laws that would permit, assist, and fund abortion was to be seen as the securing of civic rights and the social reconfiguration of the rights and power of women. The other position saw social reform as useless for women, because the issue of abortion does not in itself address a system that fails to understand women and in which women lack the right to express themselves. One did not wish, above all, to claim "civil rights" in order to undergo the violence of abortion. To be pregnant without wanting to be so or to be constrained to abort even though one wanted a child provoked conflicts in women and produced situations that no law could regulate, systematize, or resolve. This is why the simple abolishment of the criminal status of abortion, its *decriminalization*, was asked for.... One's relation to maternity and reproduction and, therefore, negatively, one's relation to abortion, could be clarified only by investigating a sexuality that had not been defined by men, by analyzing the man-woman relationship, including the motives and dynamics underlying a woman's choice to remain pregnant despite her desire to abort.[20]

It is interesting to note the return of the cultural position on the abortion law today, some thirty years after its initial approval (May 25, 1978), in the comments of a younger generation of feminists, namely, the women of the group A/Matrix Roma.

> The majority of women were not fighting for a law, but for the decriminalization of abortion. The reasoning was clear: a law would have meant that the state controlled women's bodies. And this is the way it is, because certain articles of the legal text leave room for conscientious objectors, on one hand, and for various interpretations of when and how life begins, on the other hand. This balancing act leads us

directly back to the 1970s, when women fought not for rights authorized by men, but for freedom. Today, the personal sphere has once again become the object of focus.... The Right wishes to submit women's personal freedom to the will of God, whereas the Left reduces it to a matter of rights.

Self-determination cannot exist if it is subordinated to the interests of political parties and parliamentary logic, if the law itself, once established, demands the energy of an ongoing defensive struggle whose rules are furnished by health, legal, and administrative institutions. Recent history testifies to these limitations. The aforementioned text of the law, with all of its ambiguities, is today attacked and deprived of all meaning.

The fight against abortion was a full-out war, which could not be defeated by the idea of claiming and obtaining a "right." To speak publicly about abortion carries with it a radical meaning that invites discussion about sexuality and the relationship between men and women. It means becoming conscious and reappropriating one's own body through different relations and structures, such as women's health centers. Openly discussing abortion reinvented the public and necessitated the construction of new primary institutions such as self-directed consultation offices and medical centers for women.[21]

To recognize the originality and radical nature of 1970s feminism—and its most enduring lessons, evident in today's feminist and lesbian collectives—is to recall its anomalous practices of self-help, consciousness-raising, and the exploration of the unconscious, all of which focus on a body that is investigated and narrated as the essential locus of the construction of female individuality, a body and an identity that have been shaped and dominated by the fears and desires of men, a body violated, exploited, and controlled by men, a body reduced to its sexual and reproductive functions.

At that time, female "difference" had not yet been introduced into feminist discourse; rather, women were virtually "inexistent" as a result of the effects of the "symbolic violence" perpetrated against them—a violence that led them to embody a male vision of the world, to speak the language of men, to confuse love with violence, to adapt and assimilate, as well as to painfully resist. In a passage from *Smarrirsi in pensieri lunari*, Agnese Seranis acutely summarized the "voyage" of the women's movement, undertaken at the time as a process of discovery, a project aimed at the re-appropriation of a self abstracted from nature but also confined to a "genus" or "kind":

> In every place, I found myself as inexistent; I was but a shade of their desires and needs. But I wanted to be me, I wanted to know, I wanted to hold in my hands that which I was so as to perhaps offer or exchange it. This is what I desired to give to my equals, namely, that which I was. Yet, I felt until that point only able to give my body, with which men were preoccupied and upon which they projected an image of their own desires. I understood that they only wanted to dialogue with themselves or with someone they themselves invented, someone who did not challenge their conception of life or their role in the construction of women's identity.[22]

Certain polarizations appeared in historians' reconstructions of the women's movement, such as the struggle for rights versus the struggle for full liberation. In the slogan "Change oneself and change the world," a search for connections replaced the attachment to dualisms. Participation in protests over divorce, abortion, and sexual violence was based on critical reflection and collective labor, and it was intended to ensure that the movement was not reduced to "a matter of reform," isolated from the broader discussion of sexuality and the dominance of male culture.

Feminism, precisely because it was a symptom of the shifting of the boundaries between private life and political life, between the home and the polis, found itself in what Agamben calls the "aporia" of modern democracy, that is, subject to democracy's ambiguities and contradictions.

> With *habeas corpus* (1679), the new subject of politics is no longer the human being (*homo*), but the body (*corpus*). Modern democracy is born as the vindication and exposition of this "body": one must

have a body to show.... The aporia of democracy is to wish to play out one's freedom and the happiness of human beings in the same place—bare life—which signaled humans' subjection.... Spaces, freedoms, and the rights that individuals obtained in their conflicts with centralizing powers prepared, always and at the same time, a tacit but growing inscription of their lives into the legal order.[23]

Perhaps on account of the radical nature of its practices, the impact of feminist thinking on the law was limited in Italy compared to its success in other countries. One can say that, in general, as Alessandra Facchi has remarked, the law continues to be, for feminism, "an ambiguous and controversial object";[24] it is seen both as an instrument that can help to improve the situation of women and as the most dangerous expression of male culture. In Italy, the debate has become mired in the dilemma of choosing between equality and difference, between a politics of equality and a politics characterized by tutelage and hierarchy, between the valorization of all differences and that of sexual difference, that is, a fundamentally positive and meaningful feminist value. In terms of values, models—biological, psychic, cultural—reveal their limits once they become legal norms.

Even if we disagree with the positions put forth in the book *Non credere di avere dei diritti*,[25] feminism in Italy tends to support the view that women's interests are best protected by some degree, however minimal, of legal regulation or control. Even if we recognize the symbolic reach of the law, which makes public that which is private and therefore changes our consciousness, reservations about an instrument so strongly marked by a male point of view remain, for such an instrument occludes the birth of the *unseen subject* of public life—that is, women; it fails to affirm their political existence as well as their freedom to make decisions about their own bodies and their own lives.

Beyond the Borders of Life

It is not by accident that biotechnology is being directed toward the extremes of life and death. The technologies that constitute this domain have widened the gap between life and death to the extent that the notion of immortality, formerly unthinkable as belonging to the destiny of living beings, has now achieved traction as a possibility. In their desire to be like the creator God that no longer accompanies us on our historical journey, human beings now seek to conquer the ultimate challenge: to master the beginning and the end, to rip out from nature—and from the female body—its incomprehensible center, the mystery that lies at the origin of life, to redefine the very limits of life itself.

The book that was opened by the audacious navigators of science with in vitro fertilization and, subsequently, with the mapping of the genome contains instructions not only for constructing human beings, but for tracking the entire course of their lives in order to indefinitely prolong those lives. The ability to manipulate genes—"to select genes before fertilization, to correct their actions throughout one's lifespan or even to force them to produce new tissues and organs"[26]—presented promising avenues to what had previously lain hidden and unknown. Technologies of reanimation applied to bodies in permanent vegetative states or in irreversible comas are but the latest in a series of controls, cures, and preventions that began with the primary matter of the reproductive process.

Much like a perfectible machine, a subjugated life, a life subjected to the vigilant gaze of those with dominion over this same life, such as parents, doctors, magistrates, and politicians, lacks the power to challenge or interrogate this radical reconfiguration of the human. If the human being becomes "obsolete," writes Günther Anders,[27] if it is, as it were, ejected from history and replaced by a more powerful product, namely, technology, then what forms of totalitarianism and servitude might await us in the future? The ambitious project to recreate the human, to intervene in the natural laws of evolution, is as suspect as the project that produced weapons capable of destroying the entire human species—and it seeks the same goal. The dream of regeneration, like the obsessive defense of life, health, and eternal youth, becomes, despite itself, the unsuspecting witness of dangers that threaten our very survival: the deterioration of our climate and environment, war, sickness, inequality between the rich and the poor of the world, the proliferation of the causes of death, unprecedented and relentless development.

In order to arrogate for itself the prerogatives that historically belonged to religion, techno-science today finds itself compelled to open up its laboratories to the profane public, to manage expectations and offer promises and reassurances, to engage with ethics and philosophy, and above all to confront the ineluctable relationship between the experience of embodiment and the capacity for thought shared by all individuals. The moment that the human organism becomes a "public place," an object of infinite compositions and adjustments, one emphasizes the gap between narratives that produce different kinds of knowledge, as well as that which remains unspeakable because it is shrouded in modesty and shame.

If, in the ambiguous relation between love and enmity, the body is always in some way a "stranger" to the I that inhabits it, either as master or as guest, its invasion by external agents does not render the body itself an artificial, controllable product; rather, this invasion introduces into the body elements that cannot be felt as an integral part of one's own being. The "intruder," whether a transplanted organ or a forced cohabitation with tubes, probes, or sutures, cannot but produce "disorder in one's own interiority" and necessarily transforms one's self-image, in which all is naturally held together in an "assembly of functions."

> I am open and closed. There is in me an opening through which flows an incessant stream of foreign objects: immuno-suppressant pharmaceuticals, ... the repeated check-ups all of existence placed onto a new plane, dragged from one place to another.... One becomes completely lost as one exits from the adventure. One no longer recognizes oneself: but "to recognize" no longer makes sense. One quickly becomes only an undulation, a suspension between not easily identifiable states, between pains, degrees of powerlessness, concessions.... [T]he general impression of being connected to a scale of measure, to studies, to chemical, institutional, and symbolic webs cannot be ignored.... The intruder excessively exposes me. The

intruder extrudes me, exports me, expropriates me. I am the sickness and the medicine, I am the cancerous cell and the transplanted organ, I am the immune-suppressing agent and also the remedy. I am the iron wires that hold together my sternum.... [I have] become an android of science fiction or like the living dead, as my youngest child said one day.[28]

The "beginning of mutation," which Jean-Luc Nancy described with painful lucidity on account of the experience that both prolonged his life and made him feel, at the same time, as though it had been irreversibly delivered into the hands of others, is both surprising and contradictory. The terrifying and worrisome technology that denatures and remakes nature, that is capable of both originating and destroying life, itself becomes the material of biological experimentation, an experimentation whose results are unforeseeable. Technology employs machines to protract physical survival beyond psychic and cognitive life; one thus becomes its servant, and in the case of prolonged agony, one becomes simply an appendix to it.

To the extent that they allow us to overcome the ancient dichotomies of nature-culture, body-mind, and so on, the radical changes to which our civilization, ever more uncertain of its destiny, is becoming accustomed, perplex and overwhelm us—the borders between health and sickness, life and death, immunological defense and destruction seem to have collapsed. Biology and history, natural life and individualization, these have always resisted one another, as if they belong to different orders and different value systems, as if they are organized according to an inverted hierarchy of temporal priorities in which the exercise of power, exploitation, and violence are imbricated.

Human beings have always insisted on the distance between the body—the element that they share in common with other living beings—and other beings in order to protect their essential difference, constituted by language, thought, and the capacity for creativity. But the body is also the root that generates the two sexes as members of the same species, despite their biological differences, even in the womb where distinctions between mother and child are less developed.

Perhaps this is why men, having designated themselves the sole protagonists of history, have, since the beginning of modernity, simultaneously considered women an "inferior form of life" and a "creative vortex," the depository of the divine spark, the bearer of both the promise and the menace of continuity.

Birth and death, whether seen as the limits of every singular existence or as separate realms, as uterus and tomb, or as an ideal reconnection, always refer back to the destiny that links nature and women to the dominion over women by the institutions of public life, to the dogmas and rituals of religion, to the constellation of images and symbols in the various languages of human civilization. The "question of life itself," which lies at the center of politics today, was never, from its originary relation to the city of man, its power and its laws, foreign to it.

Having finally achieved the citizenship so long denied to it, biological life seems now to have exceeded the laws and natural rights that recognized it. For all the traces that human experience has left on it, biological life today, paradoxically, is able to provide the supplement to history that fills in what is missing from textbooks and familiar narratives. No matter how abstruse the language of technology, it is not difficult to identify the conflicts about the origin of life, its evolution, its defense, and its natural end.

The shift in the power of generation has seen fathers become able to register their progeny under their own names, and today, new, ever more powerful technologies are being used to make further "progress" by pursuing the possibility of human reproduction in an artificial womb. But the dispute occasioned by this shift in power addresses not only the male appropriation of women's power, which dispenses life and death, but also the profound resistance to the acceptance of the fact that individual lives have a beginning and an end. The final end, despite our ability to delay it, is inscribed in birth; death is part of life, despite the efforts of humanity to expel it, to silence the fatality of natural law. Yet life reproduces itself endlessly, now through technologically sophisticated means, but also in savage and brutal ways. To master the genetic code and thereby hope to possess the keys to human behavior and the power to remake the human being itself, this is the triumphant rallying cry that announces each and every scientific discovery and heralds the omnipotence of the biologists, geneticists, and doctors who are seeking the path to immortality.

Few voices, either secular or religious, oppose the great changes exalted by the chorus that lauds the promise of eternal life. To think and write about death historically belonged to the poets, who were able to testify to the nothingness of existence without becoming either mute or enthralled. But we are also indebted to those writers who courageously expose themselves, who are able and willing to express our "unpresentable" passions and ultimately render silence and fragmentation bearable.

> The pathway of writing remains open. One faces pain, *souffrance*, the nothing, and one proceeds forward. One attempts this space without exhausting its limits, seeking the threshold where one can grasp an image or a sound that can be brought inside one as a precious conquest. This attempt is like the testimony of a witness, who returns from a voyage and refers to it only to begin the voyage again, not worried about whether or not the knowledge obtained is, as Baudelaire wrote, bitter.[29]

The ways of the scientist and the poet-philosopher are, of course, decisively different; they converge only in their will to penetrate the mystery of death, to mitigate its impact, its intolerability. But any story that attempts to account for the entire experience of an individual—a thinking and feeling body—risks failing to hear the whole story that lies behind the din of consoling voices, whether they champion technological progress or espouse religious fundamentalism. *The Future of an Illusion*,[30] in which Freud analyzed divine providence as an illusion arising out of the infantile need for a father, can now be seen to refer to an earthly god and is, therefore, less attractive. A fatherless society now feels itself capable of identifying with its own powerful, mechanical creatures.

The Freedom to Resemble Others

What happens when the principal preoccupation of a parent is the "success" of its child, when a mother takes her adolescent daughter to the dermatologist to have her too-thin legs "touched up," when the authoritative International Institute of Statistics' model of the future manager, described as sympathetic, determined, and attractive, is based on the infantile desires of the "dominant class"? According to Gustavo Pietropolli Charmet, in the contemporary family—increasingly a "workshop of good children" [*officina dei buoni figli*]—"the feeling of inadequacy is shifting from guilt and sin to beauty, to physical appearance, to popularity, to the role of the group."[31] Today's adolescents, described as the "children of liberty," as "belonging to the culture of risk," as "do-it-yourself types," as "completely decisive," are, at the same time, described as the "new conformists," who are launched on paths of "preordained actions" that preclude whimsy, imagination, any capacity for critique. They may be free, but only to the extent that they replicate and resemble the dominant models of beauty, efficiency, and adventurousness.

Social Darwinism, eugenics, genetic selection that favors a "superior" type of human—these are no longer the discredited and repudiated "monsters" of totalitarian ideologies or fantasies that stir up the most worrisome objectives of actual scientific experimentation. Imperceptibly, behind the avalanche of images, words, advertising and media slogans that engulfs us, the triumph of the few has become the norm. Individuation, which should have rendered every individual master of him- or herself, has, on the contrary, given way to homogenization—a flattening sameness of famous faces, temporary and fleeting media idols.

"There is no motive to remain the same, if it is possible to change for the better." This message has made cosmetic surgery one of the most popular mechanisms of transformation in the lives and social relations of individuals. But, in an inexplicable contradiction, this "change" is the result of the "fear of not appearing normal." It is necessary, therefore, to interrogate the paradox of an unprecedented freedom that is accompanied by a surfeit of impotence, by a frenzied quest for the new, all of which is imbued with a conservative angst that exalts individualism and, at the same time, longs for community.

While investigating the new form of democracy that was taking shape in North America in the nineteenth century, Alexis de Tocqueville noted that his contemporaries were "incessantly fatigued" by two contrary passions: the need for guidance and the desire to remain free—a condition that rendered individuals simultaneously "independent and weak":

> I seek to trace the novel features under which despotism may appear in the world. The first thing that strikes the observation is an innumerable multitude of men all equal and alike, incessantly endeavoring to procure the petty and paltry pleasures with which they glut their lives. Each of them, living apart, is as a stranger to the fate of all the rest—his children and his private friends constitute to him the whole of mankind; as for the rest of his fellow-citizens, he is close to them, but he sees them not—he touches them, but he feels them not; he exists but in himself and for himself alone; and if his kindred still remain to him, he may be said at any rate to have lost his country. Above this race of men stands an immense and tutelary power, which takes upon itself alone to secure their gratifications, and to watch over their fate. That power is absolute, minute, regular, provident, and mild. It would be like the authority of a parent, if, like that authority, its object was to prepare men for manhood; but it seeks on the contrary to keep them in perpetual childhood: it is well content that the people should rejoice, provided they think of nothing but rejoicing. For their happiness such a government willingly labors, but it chooses to be the sole agent and the only arbiter of that happiness: it provides for their security, foresees and supplies their necessities, facilitates their pleasures, manages their principal concerns, directs their industry, regulates the descent of property, and subdivides their inheritances—what remains, but to spare them all the care of thinking and all the trouble of living? Thus it every day renders the exercise of the free agency of man less useful and less

frequent; it circumscribes the will within a narrower range, and gradually robs a man of all the uses of himself. The principle of equality has prepared men for these things: it has predisposed men to endure them, and oftentimes to look on them as benefits.[32]

In contemporary society, which "hinders rather than destroys creativity" and in which "external forms of freedom" coexist with "regulated and tranquil servitude," what constitutes this "immense power"? In the epoch of the "personalization" of politics, in which charismatic leaders, variously said to represent Good, Evil, Civility, Barbarism, and so on, clash with one another, it is too easy to identify new "despots" and to blame them for widespread feelings of inadequacy.

In a society that believes itself to consist of equals, it is because the exception becomes the norm that it becomes necessary for this norm, which we are compelled to imitate, to possess something "common"—a generality that is recognizable and familiar.

If it is the affirmation of the individual, his or her talents, willpower, and independence from tradition that most characterizes our epoch, the locus in which one can see and measure the effects of individual success cannot but be that which generates the human being as nature and as animal, namely, the body. The new figure of authority, destined to supersede all other figures—fathers, owners, bosses, politicians—is that in which *beauty and youth* are united and which constitutes an icon of absolute control over the passage of time and over human finitude.

Contradictory feelings come into play, even if unconsciously, when we confront the mystery of the biological destiny of human beings (a "brief journey between two absences") and the expectation that science will master the principle and the indefinite prolongation of life: weakness and strength, impotence and decisiveness, shame and confidence. These contrary feelings can be said to characterize our times. But it is the limitless manipulability and transformational capacity of the material body that sustains the illusion of our being in control, despite which the tragic events of the world continue to unfold and the anxieties of an entire society persist, though this illusion appears less and less credible.

> Skin: interface, a limit, the thin layer between the inside and the outside, a mirror, a cover, a changing surface upon which one can write one's own text. Tattoos, piercings, and all other body modifications (implants, lifting, liposuction, prostheses), ... branding and scarification become ways to highlight an active subjectivity. I draw the signs on the geography of my body with body modifications that include the insertion of subcutaneous balls of steel under the skin and other kinds of surgical procedures. These modifications personalize the body, rendering it more seductive and different; they actualize and embody one's own destiny.[33]

A unique story and geography are fantastically materialized through the alteration and hybridization of the body. This story and geography are the fruit of a suspension of time and space, which are seen as obstacles to the birth of an "active subjectivity" capable of reinscribing the "text" of its own life in the empty space of memory.

"Normal" is defined by those who continuously and obsessively pursue "being in shape," both physically and psychologically. "Normal" is represented by the uniform incorporation of trends and consumer goods into the dreams of one's own uniqueness. More egregiously, war, misery, migration, religious fanaticism, and the arrogance of the powerful leave their traces on the bodies of those made to feel inadequate even while they struggle to survive.

In a society characterized by obligatory individualism, the horizon of the world inevitably shrinks until it coincides with the boundaries of the self—the skin, the senses, and the physiognomy of the face. These boundaries allow human beings to see and be seen; we are attentive to and seize on signs of confirmation or failure in the other. Language, habits, gestures, the range of expressions, all contribute to our ability to select what interests us, whether we are seeking an alternative to an anonymous existence or simply trying to keep our jobs. Uniformity and exception now belong to the same family of social relations—relations modeled on the laws of merchandising and consumption, and, hence, changeable in unforeseeable ways.

Workers have to collaborate, whether they want to or not. The attraction to numerous beauty salons is also determined by the preoccupation with one's own existence; the use of cosmetics is not always a luxury. Because of the fear of being declared no longer usable, much like outdated merchandise, men and women dye their hair and people in their forties play sports in order to remain thin.[34]

To subject the body to a regimen designed to maximize one's capacities and minimize one's inadequacies is not merely to commodify desire and the functions and social fabric of society. The body, insofar as it is indistinguishable from our being, is experienced as both internal and external; a "forced localization," it has its own laws and limits.

Before it can contend with the surrounding world, the human child must learn to control the living material that is both familiar and foreign to it, its own and that which is other to it. Insofar as the body cannot be eliminated by thought's differentiation of itself from its biological heredity, it, along with its attractive sexual powers, has never been so exalted as it is today, exploited by both business and religion, by the media and event organizers, as well as by various health agencies.

The "somewhere else" that is identified with birth and death takes its revenge after a long exile, and, perhaps, it does so in and through its own emancipation. Despite the thousand gestures, smooth and sensual curves, friendly looks, that follow us throughout our days while testifying to our eternal and irremediable inadequacy, no one seems able to recognize the "whole" individual, the living and thinking material that we are. But one can hope that this inanimate perfection might reawaken nostalgia for an imperfect past world or prefigure a more human future.

If Power Were to Become Female

When the women's movement declared that it was necessary to analyze the connections between sexuality and politics, it was not so much a call to interrogate the private lives of those men in charge of important institutions;

rather, it sought an analysis of the unequivocal fact that power has always lain in male hands and that sexuality has played a primary role in both the personal and public spheres. However, there is no doubt that when a head of state's personal life occupies the public stage, our attitude changes. This is not a matter of spying on the secrets of an individual life; rather, we are dealing here with the unexpected exposure of that which has long been hidden behind the rituals of politics—the fantasies, desires, tics, and the fears that confront every public personage, all of which have generally been confined within the walls of the home.

The avalanche of outrage that gained mass and momentum, thereby threatening the government of Silvio Berlusconi, was initiated by a family insider. The revelations that ultimately brought Berlusconi down came from the brilliant and determined woman confined to a terrain imperceptibly bordered by the positions of wife and first lady, a threshold from which it was possible to gather information about plots and unsuspected connections precisely because the separation of politics and institutional duties from emotions and domestic habits is considered absolute and sacrosanct.

Despite seeming paradoxical, the approval enjoyed by the former Italian prime minister rests for the most part on his institutional credibility. This approval derives from what communal and daily benefits he was able to preserve for the anonymous mass of citizens, which supported him because of his extreme wealth and unequalled social prestige. The seducer, seduced by his own image, by the reflection of himself in the faces of his admirers, becomes the figure, captivating to both sexes, of a masculinity that rejects female advances, a masculinity that prefers handsomeness over muscularity, wit over imperiousness, the mischievous spirit of a boy over a malicious allusion or an impertinent gesture.

The pathology to which Veronica Lario indirectly referred (describing her husband as "a man who is not well")[35] has become normalized. As normalcy, it gives form to the dreams of the greater part of men, who manifest a compulsory virility and are secretly jealous of the charm attributed to women. Proud of their female conquests, men are also sensitive to the seduction that the gynaeceum directs to its guardian and lover. According to Pierangiolo Berrettoni,

> *Homme à femme* refers to a particular psychological and behavioral type characterized by an exclusive attraction to women that is totalizing and obsessive. Perhaps it can also be described as an attraction to Woman, understood as the eternal feminine. Like romantic love, it is a form of "love" that is directed toward a particular, individual object, but it is really directed more toward a class, a category, a mental image, namely, of woman.[36]

With the pride of the warrior and the respectability of the citizen, Berlusconi, the epitome of manly strength, the incarnation of logical order (as well as the ethical and social order that separates men from women), more closely resembles Adonis, the "god of coupling," than Hercules. To disturb the ordered rituals of the polis, to arouse both the moral and political indignation of one's enemies by unscrupulous use of the law for one's own gain, by the blatant abuse of power and contempt for parliament and the judiciary, even if done secretly, expresses a constellation of masculine traits that are perceived as disarming: the sophist's ability to conjure illusion, the child's delirium of omnipotence, the use of language to capture one's listeners with words that both fascinate and deceive, divert and mislead.

Seduction is contrary to rationality and respectability, which traditional politics demands of those charged with important institutional roles. To resist seduction by appealing to truth, moral indignation, the separation between private life and public duty, inevitably produces the opposite effect to that intended: rather than restoring the dignity and integrity of politics, it unveils the sordid underbelly of politics. To employ Alberto Asor Rosa's suggestive image, it reveals "the seething, untrustworthy, rebellious sea, . . . a world of things that we have yet been unable to speak."[37]

Among the more serious "unspeakables" are the many faces of violence that have historically marked relations between the sexes—the appalling consequence of a civilization determined to emancipate the masculine from the biological limits of all living beings and furnish him with a "superiority" that he then imposes with great force on the other half of the human species. Analyses of this violence, essential for understanding the development of all known civilizations, are not lacking, and are, given the changing relations between men and women, available to all. But this very awareness, the new freedoms that have taken shape around family and community relationships, the overturning of entrenched conceptual categories and moral codes, remain at the margins of public debate, contemptuously regarded as the annoying residue of an outmoded feminism.

Believing himself to be invested with unlimited power, Berlusconi bestowed upon the pairing of politics and sexuality the most facile and superficial connection, compensating women who granted him the pleasure of their beautiful presence with the offer of the opportunity to run as candidates for his party, conceding to the female body and its charms the unusual passport of citizenship and respectability. The genuine or willful ignorance of progressive thought and practice, which have brought to light the profound political implications of the relations between men and women, individual and collectivity, biology and history, and which have attempted to melt away the thick sludge into which the public sphere is now sinking, inevitably and predictably renders the personal dimension of power no more than gossip, voyeuristic entertainment, or spectacle, or reaffirms the traditional separation, reassuring but now impractical, between body and polis, private vices and public virtues.

Chapter Two

Loving Mothers

Prisoners of a Dream

In passionate love, the "primordial breath of life" pushes lovers to find one another sufficient—an undeniably claustrophobic relation. No one is surprised if the "desire to possess or be possessed" is represented by the image of the hidden interior of the mother—that is, the womb. "The son," writes Paolo Mantegazza, "is a living member of the mother, it is flesh of the mother's flesh, blood of its blood; but even when the fruit has fallen from the branch that nourished it, it does not cease to be held within the maternal embrace. The ovary no longer embraces the child, but the loving mother herself now does so, warming it with kisses and caresses."[1]

The closed horizon of the human being's first dwelling, the absence of the word, the intrauterine quiet that does not yet know tears and separations—these are the bodily symbols of the partial indistinguishability of the originary couple of mother and child, which is accorded to adult loves; these symbols are a prison in which one feels pain only when love is lacking. Through love, human beings seek to shield themselves from death, pain, and loss, but the love that is sufficient unto itself actually serves to separate one from the world and others.

The discontent that underlies civilization, which arises from the necessary repression of our basic impulses, is no different than the temptation to deny the volcanic "mouths" that one finds at the beginning and end of each existence, namely, the uterus and the tomb. There one expects to find the full revelation of one's being, the rejoining of parts long at war—man and woman, body and mind, history and biology—in the "superhuman silence" of the organic and death. As Alberto Asor Rosa writes,

> The only moment at which two destinies seriously arrive at penetrating one another is the very same moment in which every communication fails: Great Communication requires that no communication exist. There were once two, now there is one: It seems that we have achieved the maximum identification, the maximum knowledge—but we cannot *speak* of it.[2]

As long as love remains chained to the dream of two beings melting into one, as if they were two halves of a single whole, it cannot be lived except as a terrible necessity: for women, constrained to alter their reason to live in order to justify the position of men as the sole protagonists in the world, love becomes the condition of survival. The doubt with which Pierre Bourdieu concludes his meticulous analysis of "male dominance" is less paradoxical than it seems at first glance, and it confirms the double face that love has borne throughout the centuries: anger and delight, coldness and ecstasy, fullness and annihilation. "Is love an exception—the only, if not the greatest exception—to the laws of male domination? Is love bracketed within the framework of symbolic violence? Or is love itself the subtlest, most invisible form of violence?"[3]

Is love an experience of harmony, reciprocity, and regeneration, or of confusion, self-sacrifice, and, as Sibilla Aleramo describes it, "the sacrilegious act" of forfeiting one's own individuality in the service of the other? The absoluteness that underpins these questions is, from the outset, the sign of an oppositional logic; it is an absoluteness transfixed by the allure of the ancient tale in which the divided branches of humanity are now to converge and coalesce, to splay themselves open to one another. Where such a lethal joining is a result of pressure, there can be no freedom. This tyranny of love directs those who are slaves to love to seek their lost selves in love itself.

Love of oneself and the other are born together, unaware of the distance between them, which allows them to draw borders around each other.

Continuous and reciprocally permeable with one another, the bodies of mother and unborn child become the "model of every happiness" (Freud), the instance of the greatest psychic happiness ever known, the basis of modernity's narcissistic notion that the individual is the locus of the primary social bond.

It is difficult to say to what extent the son's nostalgia for his mother's womb—the place of departure and psychic return, the first and last refuge for the world traveler—matters. Perhaps this longing for the mother is, in part, driven by women themselves on account of certain biological properties. It might also be a function of women's desire to compensate themselves for society's expropriation of their power. Relegated to the opposing sides of history, the two sexes seem to know nothing of one another but the timeless conflict that is subsumed by the illusion of falling in love, the frozen and fabricated dream of an impossible union.

Not even the indifference of productive logic and the market seem able to shake the foundations of the house shared by men and women. The couple's obsessive search for union becomes a game, spectacle, the material of scientific experimentation and online wagers, but only insofar as it pleases the public, which persistently views the female body first and foremost as an object that is trapped between the ideal of the independent, self-sufficient woman and the marred virgin of civilization.

The Vexatious Factor of Civilization

Freud's *The Unhappiness of Society*, known to us as *Civilization and Its Discontents* (1929), opens with a discussion of "oceanic feeling," which Freud's friend Romain Rolland suggested was the "authentic source of religiosity": the sense of an unlimited, unsurpassable being. Freud claimed not to have experienced such a feeling himself, but he was aware that the I, despite appearing to be "autonomous, unified, and distinct from every other being," knows various forms of trespassing. Within the I, one finds its continuity in an "unconscious psychic entity," the *Es* (Id), which "functions, so to speak, as a front"; externally, though the borders between the

I and the object tidily present themselves, one finds an "unusual state" in which things unfold in a different manner:

> At the height of being in love, the boundary between ego and object threatens to melt away. Against all the evidence of his senses, a man who is in love declares that "I" and "you" are one, and is prepared to behave as if it were a fact.[4]

Here, one recalls the beginning of life, in which the I is not yet able to distinguish between itself and the other. The image of falling in love is, hence, associated with that of the newborn. The mother-child dyad, therefore, not only underlies the image of lovers, but is sexually charged as well: the newborn attached to the mother's breast "has become the model of all love relations"; "the mother reserves for the child feelings that stem from her sexual life, expressed in caresses, kisses, cradling—the child is clearly a substitute for a sexual object."

Addressing this originary experience, which is destined to have a prolonged effect on the future development of the individual, Elvio Fachinelli says:

> Let us take the example of the relation between the small child and its mother.... The world that shapes this relation (the world of the mother—the world as mother) is a body-world (*mondo-corpo*) that is continuous with the relation and communicates with it; the body touches the child, caresses it, nourishes it. The mother can (and sometimes does not) treat the child delicately, she may or may not be hesitant with the child. The mother's body-world communicates heat, cold, balance, imbalance, pressure, contact, smells, rhythms, sounds.... This experience traces out for the child certain *basic* lines, understood as the desiring and communicating body, lines in which the universe of language becomes enmeshed. And this latter experience, which shapes the child, presupposes prior experience, that is, the symbolic presupposes those private bodily symbols.[5]

In psychic life, Freud concluded, nothing perishes; anterior stages are conserved in the final structuration. At this point, Freud abandoned the premise of religion elaborated in *The Future of an Illusion* (1927) and shifted his focus to the following question:

> Once again, only religion can answer the question of the purpose of life. One can hardly be wrong in concluding that the idea of life having a meaning stands and falls with the religious system, [sic] will therefore turn to the less ambitious question of what [sic] themselves show by their behavior to be the purpose and intention of their lives. What do they demand of life and wish to achieve in it? The answer to this can hardly be in doubt. They strive after happiness; they want to become happy and to remain so.[6]

Suffering, however, threatens human beings from all sides: from the body that is destined to perish, from the external world that rages against us with spiteful and destructive forces, and, finally, from our relations with other human beings. In the impossibility of satisfying all of their needs, human beings often seek ways to avoid their dislikes, including voluntary solitude, the use of technology to dominate nature, the sublimation of drives, the joy of artistic creation, the giving of material form to their fantasies, or the pursuit of solutions to problems or the pursuit of truth.

One might think that this latter method—the pursuit of truth—is the "finest and most elevated" way to avoid suffering, but Freud notes that, if set against the satisfaction of our most basic desires, the satisfaction afforded by such means will seem meager. For even freely chosen and satisfying work, which is certainly able to "displace a quantity of libidinal, narcissistic, aggressive and even erotic instincts," remains fundamentally linked to necessity.[7]

Freud identifies another avenue to happiness that seeks more than the mere avoidance of displeasure:

> Nor is it content to aim at an avoidance of unpleasure—a goal, as we might call it, of weary resignation; it passes this by without heed and holds fast to the original passionate striving for a positive fulfilment of happiness. And perhaps it does in fact come nearer to this goal than

any other method. I am, of course, speaking of the way of life which makes love the centre of everything, which looks for all satisfaction in loving and being loved. A psychical attitude of this sort comes naturally enough to all of us; one of the forms in which love manifests itself—sexual love—has given us our most intense experience of an overwhelming sensation of pleasure and has thus furnished us with a pattern for our search for happiness. What is more natural than that we should persist in looking for happiness along the path on which we first encountered it? The weak side of this technique of living is easy to see; otherwise no human being would have thought of abandoning this path to happiness for any other. It is that we are never so defenceless against suffering as when we love, never so helplessly unhappy as when we have lost our loved object or its love.[8]

Most difficult to overcome is the kind of suffering caused by those social institutions that regulate the reciprocal relations of human beings in the family, the state, and society. The heaviest burden comes from the restrictions imposed by society upon individuals in the name of society's ideals. We must interrogate civilization, then, about its incompatibility with happiness.

Nonetheless, human beings have made great progress at fulfilling their "fabulous desires" through technology and science, becoming almost godlike in the process.

Man has, as it were, become a kind of prosthetic God. When he puts on all his auxiliary organs he is truly magnificent; but those organs have not grown onto him and they all give him much trouble at times. Nevertheless, he is entitled to console himself with the thought that this development will not come to an end precisely with the year 1930 A.D. Future ages will bring with them new and probably unimaginably great advances in this field of civilization and will increase man's likeness to God still more. But in the interests of our investigations, we will not forget that present-day man does not feel happy in his Godlike character.[9]

The distinctive characteristic of civilization, besides the veneration of the highest psychic, intellectual, scientific, and artistic qualities, is the "way in which reciprocal relations between human beings—whether as neighbors, as helpmates, as one another's sexual objects, or as members of a family and the state"—are regulated.

> Sublimation of instinct is an especially conspicuous feature of cultural development; it is what makes it possible for higher psychical activities, scientific, artistic or ideological, to play such an important part in civilized life. If one were to yield to a first impression, one would say that sublimation is a vicissitude which has been forced upon the instincts entirely by civilization.[10]

Accordingly, Freud attempted to understand the forces that gave rise to the evolution of society and the reasons for the conflict between the civilizing process of society and the primordial desires of human beings.

> The fateful process of civilization would thus have set in with man's adoption of an erect posture. From that point the chain of events would have proceeded through the devaluation of olfactory stimuli and the isolation of the menstrual period to the time when visual stimuli were paramount and the genitals became visible, and thence to the continuity of sexual excitation, the founding of the family and so to the threshold of human civilization. This is only a theoretical speculation, but it is important enough to deserve careful checking with reference to the conditions of life which obtain among animals closely related to man.[11]

The family, then, structures itself in terms of two pairs: a man who appropriates for himself a woman as sexual object, and the mother who appropriates the child for herself. The foundation that underlies our life in common is twofold—love and work.

> The communal life of human beings had, therefore, a two-fold foundation: the compulsion to work, which was created by external

necessity, and the power of love, which made the man unwilling to be deprived of his sexual object—the woman—and made the woman unwilling to be deprived of the part of herself which had been separated off from her—her child. *Eros* and *Ananke* [Love and Necessity] have become the parents of human civilization too.[12]

Procuring maximum satisfaction for human beings, sexual love thus becomes the model of all happiness: genital eroticism becomes the center of life itself. As a result, however, human beings become psychologically dependent upon the external world, that is, on the selected love object. Some individuals defend themselves against this dependency by renouncing all sexual satisfaction and dedicating themselves to a sublimated love that embraces everyone. But according to Freud, a love that refuses to choose is less valuable.

People give the name "love" to the relation between a man and a woman whose genital needs have led them to found a family; but they also give the name "love" to the positive feelings between parents and children, and between the brothers and sisters of a family, although we are obliged to describe this as "aim-inhibited love" or "affection." Love with an inhibited aim was in fact originally fully sensual love, and it is so still in man's unconscious. Both—fully sensual love and aim-inhibited love—extend outside the family and create new bonds with people who before were strangers. Genital love leads to the formation of new families, and aim-inhibited love to "friendships" which become valuable from a cultural standpoint because they escape some of the limitations of genital love, as, for instance, its exclusiveness.[13]

Love, then, is seen as one of the foundational elements of society. But Freud paused to reflect on the fact that this correlation between love and civilized society, during the course of evolution, is clear:

On the one hand love comes into opposition to the interests of civilization; on the other, civilization threatens love with substantial restrictions.

This rift between them seems unavoidable. The reason for it is not immediately recognizable. It expresses itself at first as a conflict between the family and the larger community to which the individual belongs. We have already perceived that one of the main endeavours of civilization is to bring people together into large unities. But the family will not give the individual up. The more closely the members of a family are attached to one another, the more often do they tend to cut themselves off from others, and the more difficult is it for them to enter into the wider circle of life. The mode of life in common which is phylogenetically the older, and which is the only one that exists in childhood, will not let itself be superseded by the cultural mode of life which has been acquired later. Detaching himself from his family becomes a task that faces every young person, and society often helps him in the solution of it by means of puberty and initiation rites. We get the impression that these are difficulties which are inherent in all psychical—and, indeed, at bottom, in all organic—development.

Furthermore, women soon come into opposition to civilization and display their retarding and restraining influence—those very women who, in the beginning, laid the foundations of civilization by the claims of their love. Women represent the interests of the family and of sexual life. The work of civilization has become increasingly the business of men, it confronts them with ever more difficult tasks and compels them to carry out instinctual sublimations of which women are little capable. Since a man does not have unlimited quantities of psychical energy at his disposal, he has to accomplish his tasks by making an expedient distribution of his libido. What he employs for cultural aims he to a great extent withdraws from women and sexual life. His constant association with men, and his dependence on his relations with men, even estrange him from his duties as a husband and father. Thus the woman finds herself forced into the background by the claims of civilization and she adopts a hostile attitude towards it. . . .

> ... In this respect civilization behaves towards sexuality as a people or a stratum of its population does which has subjected another one to its exploitation. Fear of a revolt by the suppressed elements drives it to stricter precautionary measures.... But heterosexual genital love, which has remained exempt from outlawry, is itself restricted by further limitations, in the shape of insistence upon legitimacy and monogamy. Present-day civilization makes it plain that it will only permit sexual relationships on the basis of a solitary, indissoluble bond between one man and one woman, and that it does not like sexuality as a source of pleasure in its own right and is only prepared to tolerate it because there is so far no substitute for it as a means of propagating the human race.[14]

The conflict between eros and civilized society, as we shall see, depends not only on the restrictions that civilization imposes upon our basic impulses, but also on the fact that society's determination to unite the greatest number of individuals clashes with the essence of the individual—its originary form—which precedes eros and aims to "make one more than one alone." Once this aim is achieved, eros wishes to go no further: the love dyad is sufficient unto itself.

> But civilization demands other sacrifices besides that of sexual satisfaction. We have treated the difficulty of cultural development as a general difficulty of development by tracing it to the inertia of the libido, to its disinclination to give up an old position for a new one. We are saying much the same thing when we derive the antithesis between civilization and sexuality from the circumstance that sexual love is a relationship between two individuals in which a third can only be superfluous or disturbing, whereas civilization depends on relationships between a considerable number of individuals. When a love-relationship is at its height there is no room left for any interest in the environment; a pair of lovers are sufficient to themselves, and do not even need the child they have in common to make them happy.

In no other case does Eros so clearly betray the core of his being, his purpose of making one out of more than one; but when he has achieved this in the proverbial way through the love of two human beings, he refuses to go further.

So far, we can quite well imagine a cultural community consisting of double individuals like this, who, libidinally satisfied in themselves, are connected with one another through the bonds of common work and common interests.[15]

In *On Narcissism: An Introduction* (1914), Freud delineated this infantile or prehistoric feature of love even more clearly.

With respect to the child's object choice (or the growing individual's choice), we see how the child is drawn to the first sexual objects with which it experiences satisfaction. The first sexual satisfaction of an autoerotic nature is experienced in relation to those vital functions that are aimed at survival. Sexual impulses first rest upon the satisfaction of I impulses, and only later do they become independent. This "resting upon" is evident in the fact that the first sexual objects are those persons that nourish, care for, and protect the baby, namely, the mother or other primary caregiver.

... In a love relationship, not feeling loved diminishes the sense of self, whereas feeling loved increases the sense of self.... A person in love is humble. One who loves loses, as it were, a part of their own narcissism, which can only be recovered if one is loved in return. It seems that, in each of these relations, the feeling of self is maintained through the relation with the narcissistic dimension of a love relationship....

... Love itself, like the breath of life as well as privation, suppresses the feeling of self; to be loved, to have one's love returned, to possess the love object, is to be raised up.... The return to the I of the objectivated libido and its transmutation into narcissism represent in a certain way the restoration of a happy love. Moreover, a true and proper happy love corresponds to the originary situation in which it is not possible to distinguish between the libido for the object and the libido of the I.[16]

Narcissism, Freud concluded, is the originary dwelling of the libido, its general neighborhood.

At this point, Freud might have deepened his analysis of the "disturbing" element that lies behind eros, that "originary breath of life" that should have remained hidden, which, reappearing in adult sexuality, threatens the individuality and social bonds of the male. In his essay "The Uncanny" (1919), Freud intuited that the uncanny (*unheimlich*) refers to something that nests in something known and familiar (*heimisch*); it is the face that must remain hidden. The distant, prehistoric antecedent of eros, then, is love in its primary form of narcissism, which, reappearing in adult relationships, becomes dangerous: it violates individuality and threatens to overtake it.

The dyad of love, the unity of two, the fused couple, contains within itself the powerful potential for destruction. Behind the house of the adult lies the first abode, namely, the mother's womb. The nostalgia that transforms coitus into a return to the womb brings with it the possibility of the loss of separateness, the risk of becoming indistinct. By transforming woman into mother, the male assures for himself continuity with the body that activated both *hunger* and *love*, but this continuity also condemns him to live with the "disturbing" though familiar something (the uncanny).

In this experience, love and hate, eros and thanatos, are interwoven and almost indistinguishable:

> It often happens that neurotic individuals perceive female genitalia as disturbing. This uncanniness (*etwas Unheimliches*) provides, however, access to the ancient homeland (*Heimat*) of human beings, to one's first abode, the place in which everyone dwelled for a time. As the saying goes, "Love is nostalgia." And when one thinks "this place is familiar, I have been here before" while dreaming, the dream

landscape is the dream's substitution for the genital organs or the mother's body. Even in this case, then, *Unheimliches* was once *heimisch* (home), familiar. The German prefix *un* denotes more than a negation; it signifies the opposite of a removal.[17]

At this point, Freud, who remained faithful to his idealized vision of the mother-child relation—"the unique site of ambivalence"—sought another explanation. Failing to recognize that the capacity to destroy is born from within this repetition of eros in its originary form, he looked outward and linked it to an external factor, proposing the hypothesis of the "death drive" as a basic, originary, and independent drive that stands alongside and opposes eros. The human being is not domesticated; rather, it is moved by something other than love—that is, by an aggressive impulse that is also part of the most tender of relations, including those between mother and child.

> In abolishing private property we deprive the human love of aggression of one of its instruments, certainly a strong one, though certainly not the strongest; but we have in no way altered the differences in power and influence which are misused by aggressiveness, nor have we altered anything in its nature. Aggressiveness was not created by property. It reigned almost without limit in primitive times, when property was still very scanty, and it already shows itself in the nursery almost before property has given up its primal, anal form; it forms the basis of every relation of affection and love among people (with the single exception, perhaps, of the mother's relation to her male child).[18]

Here, Freud locates the struggle not within eros, but between two interwoven and opposing powers that cannot be mistaken for one another. In such a formulation, one can only hope that eros will be victorious.

In *Civilization and Its Discontents*, Freud draws closer to the discovery of the violence embedded within love, a prehistoric heritage that human beings carry within themselves—namely, the originary nostalgia for the unity of two-in-one. Violent is the male's appropriation of the female body, from which he receives care and sexual stimulation. Violent, too, is the *dream of love*, understood as the fusion of two beings into one, the reconfiguration of the male conception of men and women as a sort of *blurred doubling* (*sdoppiamento*). The death drive is manifest in the temptation to drown in the beatitude of the release of tension and, hence, in life itself. Aggression is necessary to preserve this *ideal unity*, to expel whatever threatens this unity. The same can be said, of course, about the search for union by *groups* and *nations*.

Much like the repetition of the originary breath of life, violence is contained within eros itself; in love and violence we find the *logic of war*—the undeclared war between the sexes that encompasses the male's appropriation of the female body, the fixation of women on the role of motherhood, women's expulsion from the historical community of men, which regards itself as homogeneous with its own genealogy. We can speak here of "sexual cleansing," that is, the negation by males of their heterogeneous origin.

The historical community, in turn, was unable to avoid the analogous movements of communalization and closure, inclusion and division. The ties that make men visible in private as husband, son, and lover, sometimes, and with greater intensity, transfer themselves into the public sphere, especially when the life of the group seems to be threatened.

According to James Hillman, "The intensity of the love for war is born from a collapse. The desperation of a life experienced together comprises the love for those few with whom we dwell, a love that exceeds eating, pissing, and sleeping together."[19] Where a community of persons is constituted as an organic unity—whether in war and nationalism, in identity-based constructs, in ethnic fortresses, in the absolutization of difference—one can hypothesize that union with the mother, an imaginary and exclusive model of love that regards openness and diversity as a threat, has been reactivated and reproduced. This is why nationalism appeals to women. The "birth" of a nation may be the birth of a patriarchal genealogy, but it also recalls an organic cohesion, a total and mystical unity connected to the maternal body.

One finds here the mother-homeland (*madre-patria*) and even the motherland (*matria*): a male agenda disguised as the female body. In this conception, the restoration of the traditional roles of mother and wife are restored, and this metaphor of the family situates men as fathers, sons, and lovers. If the nation is a male idea, it nonetheless incarnates itself in a feminine figure that is not only a symbol, but a "mute effigy."

With his discussion of the link between love and hate, Freud began to grasp the "vexatious factor" that inserts itself into civilized society and the relations between individuals and peoples. This link originated in the "first abode" that the male did not wish to abandon; thereby relegating women to the position of mothers, men appropriated for themselves woman's generative body and designated love as the center of her life. To safeguard eros in its prehistoric form—the only form that, according to Freud, can bring us happiness, Freud was constrained to displace aggression onto an external factor and thus hypothesized the death drive (thanatos) as equal and contrary to eros.

In Freud's correspondence with Einstein (1932), the latter asked, "Is there a way to free human beings from the fatality of war?" In his response, Freud began to take a less dichotomous view of the relationship between love and hate. It is the very mixing of love and hate, preservation and destruction, life and death that made the identification of these drives so difficult. And this difficulty also obtains in our personal and social lives, in the relations between the sexes, and groups, nations, and so forth. Just as the logic of war is internal to the structure of eros, so hate contains love within itself.

War, which almost always accompanies the birth of a nation and many of its most important events, destroys and expels, but always in order to gather together and protect. It is here that Freud began to understand love and hate as more intertwined than opposing.

> Love and hate, conservation and destruction, are less separate than one might think.... War as a sacrificial duty, even though it essentially absolves combatants for all acts of destruction, signifies for human beings destruction in the service of the conservation of what one loves.[20]

Perhaps, then, with greater awareness, we can undo the bedeviling knot that we know as the "humanitarian war."

The consciousness that has been missing from the millennium-long naturalization of the unequal relation between the sexes can today reintroduce into history, that is, into culture and politics, other enigmatic, heretofore unspoken knots, including first and foremost those that have, until now, impeded the radical discussion of various relations by obscuring the imaginary that underlies them, especially the knots of life and death, love and violence. Even though it remains distant, we can see here the beginning of the end of a ruinous legacy. Have we, perhaps, arrived at the end of the "dialectic"?

The Vile Body

Using facile symbols that appeal to common sense, politics always seeks to simplify, proclaim, and blame. The undeclared war on female sexuality, which signals the dominance of the historical community of men, has left enduring traces in the lives of individuals and in society, in cultures and the institutions of public life, in daily habits and the histories of peoples. Rape and murder are extreme forms of sexism, and it is a mistake to consider them separately, for they belong to a continuous history of relations of patriarchal power and culture in which, despite constitutions, laws, and the trumpeted values of democracy, women are barely recognized as "persons." Women continue to be defined in terms of a sexual and procreative function. Unfortunately, many women have internalized this definition of womanhood out of the need to adapt and survive in a male-dominated world. The female body ensures pleasure, care, and the continuation of the species. It is no accident, then, that one of the great causes of concern for a society in crisis, a society engulfed by wave after wave of immigrants and awash in hatred of other peoples, is the denaturing (*denaturalità*) of the individual.

It is important, therefore, that the violability of the female body—its penetrability and susceptibility to murder—not be conceived as belonging to the natural order; it should not be seen as an inherent consequence of a momentary *rampage* of madness or of backward, foreign, "barbaric" customs. Rather, the violability of the female body belongs to history, to our Graeco-Roman-Christian history. The violability of the female body is a function of the birth of the polis, of the sexualized division of labor, of the separation between home and city, family and state. The annihilation of woman as a person, as an individual and political subject, inevitably produces the debasement of the female body and its association with other "vile bodies"—those of the adolescent, the prisoner, the slave—over whom men have wielded, since the beginning of modernity, the sovereign power of life and death.

The ideologies and habits of the political class, and the intellectuals who court it, have not changed over time. The extension of citizenship to women, who have, until recently, been considered "imperfect," has not eradicated the view of the feminine as lack, as subhuman, as weakness that requires protection (from its own impulses as well as the larger world) and guidance. If emancipation is viewed as repulsive by women, even by those who desired it, it is because this emancipation was configured as flight from a devalued, insignificant femininity—a femininity subordinate to the vision of the world that produced it. Hence, Paolo Mantegazza's nineteenth-century definition of the emancipated woman does not seem outdated:

> This new freedman of modern society is tolerated but is not equal to us. She is like an orphan who lives with a family but is not an integral part of it. She becomes a concubine and then a mother, but a great step needs to be taken before she can become a woman or, in other words, a female-male, a most noble and delicate creature, who thinks and feels like a woman and in so doing completes us.[21]

What is the "feminization" of work and politics if not the extension of the traditional domestic role to the public sphere, the calling upon a reserve of female energy by a civilization in decline?

To combat violence today means to face the problem at its root: we must drive out the cultural assumptions, incarnated in institutions, in the conditions of work, in morality, in the images that pervade television and advertising, in the unwritten norms of tradition and conventional wisdom, that produce violence. It means, above all, that we must recognize, across all ideologies, that the family continues to be exalted as refuge, security, and the guarantee of healing and comfort at the same time that daily newspapers across the globe report the broken bones and bruises inflicted by men on women's bodies—wounds that serve as a testament to the perverse link between love and hate and that demonstrate the cost of women's autonomy. One can easily kill a woman whose independence and immense strength one fears and whose freedom to live her own life and use her own body and capacities in any way she likes one finds intolerable. The continuing repression of women—the most ancient form of domination in the world—undoubtedly has to do with the material, public, and symbolic turmoil that feminist awareness has produced.

"Without our intervention," wrote Virginia Woolf almost a century ago, "no one would have been able to pacify these waters, and these fertile lands would still be a desert. We have given birth, raised, washed, and taught, until they reach six or seven years of life, the 1.62 billion human beings that, according to statistics, populate the earth."[22]

Violence against women, which mostly occurs in the home at the hands of fathers, husbands, and lovers, does not bespeak a natural or divine order to which one must yield; neither does it bespeak a freedom to respond in kind or to defend oneself. Men almost always become violent when confronted with separation. They rage and sometimes kill when their sexual advances are refused. Do they kill because of the threat of abandonment? Do they kill because women's freedom imposes limits on them? Or do they kill because they find themselves, for the first time, at the mercy of needs and dependencies that had hitherto been hidden or assuaged?

If today's violence signifies a rebellion that has been simmering for decades as a result of female consciousness, which, freed from internalized models of womanhood, has disrupted the long-standing equilibrium between men and women, it may be because women can increasingly be found on both sides of the border that separates the private from the public sphere. Domestic violence continues to be reported as a simple fact in the daily news, but by examining the statistics and making inquiries of this fact, one can determine the extent and nature of the violence. Rape and murder that take place in the streets and the open spaces of the city, when not misrepresented and misattributed by the campaigns against foreigners, reveal the interior of the family and its internal relations, from which a destructive fury emerges.

The political forces that responded with indifference or hostility to the feminist revolution of the 1970s, which discovered the political nature of the body and the person, are constrained, despite themselves and by the risk of even greater irrelevance, to interrogate the underpinnings of the power that men have arrogated for themselves in public life. These forces must ask whether the greatest and most unjustifiable violence today is the silence and indifference that cloak the domination now revealed in its extended form.

The ancient and savage residue of domination, which has woven itself into the social fabric to the extent that it has disappeared from our consciousness, paradoxically reemerges when women advance toward emancipation. The demand for an equal female presence wherever and whenever decisions are made requires the criticism of every sort of fundamentalism, the discussion of the centrality of work and *operaismo*[23] in the politics of the Left, and the rethinking of all dualisms, beginning with those that oppose and render complementary female and male, biology and history, individual and society.

There are those who read this reappearance of male domination as regression and barbarization of the relation between the sexes. I prefer to think that, rather than a return of the same, we are dealing here with the recovery of an eclipsed "prehistory" whose return has the power to unsettle society's unexplored depths and open it up to a different consciousness and a still-coming-to-be female freedom.

LIBERATED OR PROSTITUTED BODIES?

The body, in its vicissitudes from birth to the end of life, is always the object of the powers and conceptions of public life: the state, the church, medicine, biotechnology, morality, and so on. As a biological entity, the body is reducible to the sum of its organs; as "bare life" (*nuda vita*), it is exposed to war, hunger, disease, and migration. The body has been put to work in slave-like conditions and forced into shape (by plastic surgery, fitness regimes, diets, etc.), flattened by fashion and advertising. One might say, then, that the body is emerging from the shadows and taking its *revenge*, but the very moment that it appears on the public scene, it becomes obvious that history has left its marks upon it; it has been devalued and its distorted form naturalized. The body has become a body-object, merchandise, an object of consumption—a body far removed from the embodied I sought by the antiauthoritarian movements of the 1970s.

The presence of women in public life—at work, in the professions, in politics, and so on—has increased significantly. Interpretations and analyses of this presence are many, but almost all are framed within a traditional point of view as dealing with "the female question." These analyses discuss the advantages and disadvantages of this presence, issues of discrimination, and the advance of equality as if women were a minority or an "imperfect citizenry." Newspapers present immense amounts of data on work, careers, underused female talent, the contributions of women to businesses and corporations, maternity leave, and so on. But one rarely asks why young women seem uninterested in changing this state of affairs. The most radical elements of feminism never opted to fight for rights, laws, or integration into a society created by men according to their own standards.

The dream was more ambitious: to redefine the economy and politics on the basis of what had been rejected, confined to the private realm, defined as belonging to nature—that is, the body and the person. Today, the dreams of the new generation seem to be oriented in a different direction: young women look, on one hand, to the images of women in television and advertising (showgirls, models, et al.) and, on the other hand, they struggle to reconcile motherhood with a professional career.

The female body today is both the *erotic body* and the *maternal body*, the latter understood not merely as the desire for motherhood but also as the valorization of "female gifts"—a feature of the new economy's system of production. In research carried out at the Università Bocconi, this view of what women bring to the public sphere is referred to as *Value W*. More generally, one can say that it is the feminine itself, as traditionally defined by the attributes assigned to it—attributes now regarded as a precious resource for the economic system—that blurs the border between private and public and, therefore, between the destinies of women and men. Precariousness, fluidity, relational capacities, emotions, imaginaries—to the extent that public space, work, and politics have been "feminized," these are now the characteristic traits of our times.

The recent debates about showgirls, escorts, and sexualized images of women, especially about the representation of women on television and in advertising, arose in response to events surrounding Silvio Berlusconi. The connection between Berlusconi and the representation of women lies in the shift, facilitated by the promise of political favors, of female figures (many of them procured for Berlusconi) from the entertainment world to that of political candidacy. The notoriety of the protagonist, his habits unmasked by the public declarations of his wife, Veronica Lario, as well as the statements of certain escorts, have exposed an essential aspect of the power relations between the sexes, which Paolo Tabet calls "the sexual-economic" exchange.[24]

The perennial relation between sex and politics becomes apparent at the moment private events erupt into the highest offices of the state; it is here, precisely in the connection between the personal and public spheres, that the political meaning of the commodification of the female body encounters a new form of obfuscation that results in a political clash, moral indignation, or scandal.

The question thus arises: What kinds of bodies are at play today? Are they the *liberated bodies* of women who have taken control of their own lives and use their bodies as they like or are they prostituted, commercialized bodies? Do these bodies signify a change in the relations of power between the sexes or do they confirm these relations? Do we see here the new subjectivity sought by feminism or a renewed objectification of women? Are these bodies victims, heroines, or something else entirely? What changes in the historical, political, and cultural context have led to the current revival of feminism?

The shifting of the borders between the body and the polis that took place in 1968 produced "unforeseen political subjects"—youth and women—and together they identified and clarified problems linked to the relation between biology and history and between the individual and the collectivity. This newfound clarity ought to have enabled us to abandon dualisms such as male and female.

The impression of what is happening today is of an overturning: the body, sexuality, and personal life are no longer the repressed of history; rather, they have entered the heart of history as protagonists. The ancient separation between private and public has fallen away, and we are moving toward an amalgamation in which it is difficult to disentangle the two. When the prime minister of Italy treats institutional issues as if they were the administrative problems of his own corporations, thus merging politics with his own person, we can say that the private has devoured the public.

But we also have an opposite impression: every intimate corner of our lives is regulated by the outside world, shaped by our consumption, by advertising. Our bodies, sexuality, and intimate lives are the matter that feeds the media. The danger is not only that we become unable to narrate our own experience, but that we may become unable to "experience" anything at all when public discourse dominates all experience in all places.

Given this hybrid and undifferentiated mix of archaic ideas and the postmodern acceleration of change in contemporary society, we find aptness in Alexis de Tocqueville's concluding reflections in *Democracy in America*:

> I think then that the species of oppression by which democratic nations are menaced is unlike anything which ever before existed in the world: our contemporaries will find no prototype of it in their memories. I am trying myself to choose an expression which will accurately convey the whole of the idea I have formed of it, but in vain; the old words "despotism" and "tyranny" are inappropriate: the thing itself is new; and since I cannot name it, I must attempt to define it.[25]

The "immense and protecting power" to which a "crowd of equals" is drawn, seeking only to procure for its members small and vulgar pleasures

—the same power that fixes them "immediately in infancy"—is no different than the figure of the "deadly mother" who both satisfies and devours, and which, according to Elvio Fachinelli, underlies and drives our consumer society.[26]

Centralization and popular sovereignty, rule by one, and the omnipotence of the majority, alongside regulated slavery, the need to be guided, and the desire to remain free: are these not the hallmarks of "Berlusconism," from which it is so difficult to disentangle oneself?

In the last few years, ambiguous female figures have emerged—showgirls, escorts, models—figures that, though their bodies have been commodified and their sexuality exchanged for cash or careers, cannot, strictly speaking, be considered prostitutes. We cannot properly speak of "victims" here—at least, not in terms of contemporary models of victimhood—insofar as these women champion and exploit the terms by which men have defined them. Indeed, throughout history, women have attempted to turn the "reasons" for their minority status to their own advantage. But this use of the body is not the reclaiming of the female body and sexuality that feminists advocated in the 1970s. Rather, we see here a form of emancipation, though it may be perverse and questionable. The idea of the "feminine" as such has been emancipated, and it takes its *revenge* by emerging into the public sphere and profiting from the demands and desires of the market, of business and industry, of show business, and from the exchange of favors between men.

Drawing upon Virginia Woolf's insights in "Thoughts on Peace in an Air Raid" (1941), we might best define these ambiguous female figures as willing, gladsome slaves (*schiave radiose*). As English men, wrote Woolf, fought in the skies against an "unconscionable Hitlerism" dedicated to dominion and aggression, women gazed upon their reflections in shop windows: "powdered women, disguised women, women with red lips and nails . . . slaves who [sought] to make others slaves." She concluded, "If we could liberate ourselves from slavery, we would have liberated men from tyranny. Hitlers are generated from slaves."[27] Both men and women obey "instincts encouraged and nourished by education and tradition," and this pertains equally to male aggression and maternal instinct. We seek to open up new possibilities for creative power in both sexes, but men must give up their arms and women must not be restricted to the exercise of motherhood.

Virginia Woolf clearly encapsulated the contradiction in which women found themselves: imaginatively exalted, historically insignificant, praised for their beauty and motherly talents—seductresses and mothers. In either case, women were identified with the body, a body defined by its sexual functions in relation to the only sex recognized as possessing an I—individuality, moral will, language, power, the right to speak on behalf of both sexes. The place of women—as mother, wife, or prostitute—was assigned to them by men.

The female body, understood as the body that generates and provides sexual pleasure, renders women powerful in the eyes of men. As the male myth of women has it, these "powerful" women pushed men to assert their dominion and control, assuring men that strong, attractive women were made so for the sake of men's interests, in order to make life good for men. One finds an overturning at the origin of the relation between the sexes that made the "weak" into the "masters."

Rousseau perfectly describes this relation in *Émile*, in which he specified the position of women in the social contract:

> She is dependent on our feelings, on the price we put upon her value, and the opinion we have of her charms and her virtue. Nature has decreed that woman, both for herself and her children, should be at the mercy of man's judgment.... The children's health depends in the first place on the mother's, and the early education of man is also in woman's hands; his morals, his passions, his tastes, his pleasures, his happiness itself, depend on her. A woman's education must therefore be planned in relation to men. To be pleasing in his sight, to win his respect and love, to train him in childhood, to tend him in manhood, to counsel and console, to make his life pleasant and happy, these are the duties of woman for all time, and this is what she should be taught while she is young. The further we depart from this principle, the further we shall be from our goal, and all our precepts will fail to

secure her happiness.... The man should be strong and active; the woman should be weak and passive; the one must have both the power and the will; it is enough that the other should offer little resistance.[28]

Thus far, the relation between the sexes has not been investigated as fully as it should be. Although expressed in somewhat different terms, the discussion of this relation has been taken up in our own times by the feminist economist Antonella Picchio:

> What destroys women is not the strength of men, but their weakness. Patriarchs have never been able to stand on their own two feet alone; this is why they constructed a patriarchal system of control over women's bodies and minds. It is not only the practices and symbols of the patriarchal system that oppress us, but also our assumption of responsibility for the quality of life of our friends and children. We suffer from the delirium of omnipotence and they suffer grave weaknesses that remain hidden from us.[29]

In a few "fragments of clear intuition" that vividly illustrate the interior experience of women, Sibilla Aleramo noted:

> Intimate desire to dedicate oneself to another, pleasure in giving oneself over to the beloved without asking for anything in return.
>
> An internal self-deprecation and exaggerated concern for the oppressor, love and hate together...
>
> ...Why do we adore sacrifice in motherhood? Where does this inhuman idea of motherly sacrifice come from?
>
> I was now a slave to my own strength, to my creative imagination. My own power consisted in making life good.... My strength lay in the preservation of such a power, even if it meant that, from my own perspective, I gave up on all illusions. Love without a why, as if without a subject.
>
> I do not succeed in finding my own interior freedom, the obligation to exist for myself. I need to be necessary for another living

creature in order to live. Love is like this; it is the attachment to a person whom one thinks is necessary. For women, this is love. For eight years, I gave everything, my all, to Franco. I performed this sacrilegious act from the perspective of my own individuality.

I could not wholly take into account all of his needs, prevent and satisfy them. I was miserable if I did not succeed in doing so, especially because I had decided to sacrifice my individuality, to forget myself, to give all of my energy to the individuality that was being formed next to me.[30]

To understand the depth of the conviction that a woman's duty is to serve a man, to make a good life for him, one need only read the assessments of Aleramo by two well-known men, Benedetto Croce and Emilio Cecchi. "I am not a cheap moralist," says Croce. "I understand and excuse the error, caused by the passion of youthful sensuality and fantasy, of your abandonment of your husband and child.... But the deed was done, and you had an excellent chance to create a new life when you were with Cena. You wanted, however, to love Cena, but your duty was to sacrifice yourself to him." Responding to Aleramo's abandonment of her family, Cecchi remarked, "No maternal servitude or unconditional gift could ... negate you. All you need is yourself."[31]

To fulfill the obligation of living for oneself, to legitimately live one's own life remains almost impossible for women. It is very difficult to mitigate the sense of responsibility that women feel for children, husbands, and family members in general. Time for oneself must vie with feelings of guilt in those who have internalized the care of others as their natural destiny.

Let us turn back to the figures of the mother and the prostitute. The erotic body is almost always met with contempt, which is clearly evident in the degrading images of the feminine that pervade television and advertising. We see less contempt in newspaper articles about the economy and the exalted talents of women, their capacity for relationship-building and the mediation of conflict, their adaptability, and so forth. The rhetoric of motherhood is used to justify the fact that the system of production exploits women for the very same work performed in the home for free.

In the 1970s, femininity was critically analyzed for the way in which it was defined in relation to men and in the service of men. As feminists, we did not speak of the "valorization of differences"; rather, we addressed the notion of difference and the need to dispense with all forms of dualism. We discovered that "differences" are the product of an abstraction of a process of differentiation that flows through every individual, a deforming abstraction that ultimately separates aspects of the person that are, in fact, indistinguishable—for example, body and thought, sensation and reason. The discussion of differences led us to realize that these differences had been polarized into opposites that were then framed as complementary and ordered hierarchically, from superior to inferior. It became clear that "differences of kind" (differences between species), as they were understood at the time, constituted the symbolic foundation of a relation of power that underpinned all dualities: woman/man, biology/history, individual/society, among others.

The experiences of female managers, recorded in Luisa Pogliana's *Donna senza guscio: Percorsi femminili in azienda* [Women without shells: Female paths in the world of business],[32] clearly demonstrate the contradictions encountered by women who believed they could modify the organization of work and the exercise of power by drawing upon their "female competencies"—that is, the capacities and skills that are rooted in motherhood and the care of the home. Moreover, only women are required to reconcile, and reunite in themselves, as an internalized ideal, the demands of life (love and motherhood), work, personal relationships, and professional responsibilities.

Many of the difficulties and disappointments that women encounter are born from the ambiguity implicit in the "valorization of differences," an ambiguity that promotes an illusion of reciprocity between the sexes that is based on opposite characteristics, on hidden relations of power rooted in gender stereotypes—not only the domination of men over women and of history over nature, but also the *sexual division of labor*—a false reciprocity between the domestic domain of women and the public domain of men.

Women have been subjected to patriarchy both within the family and outside of it. One might wonder whether women were tempted, in the private sphere, to exercise their power in their dominion over their children and in "taking care of" perfectly healthy men. Seduction and motherhood, deeply entrenched in the relations of love and domestic life, also find purchase in the workplace. The marriage of the "maternal code" and the "erotic code" make it difficult to change the relations of power; it is easier to manipulate them, which, of course, serves the economic system of production rather than the interests of women. The exercise of these codes in the workplace—codes inspired by love and care, which cannot be monetized—risks doubling the free and invisible work already being done in the home.

Another interesting feature of patriarchy is the flexibility and adaptability of its precepts. We find a unique overlap between one element of the feminist agenda and changes that have occurred in the economy and politics as a result of the shrinking border between the private and public spheres. The prevalence of immaterial and cognitive labor in contemporary production requires the female "talent" of forging relationships, much vaunted as essential for innovation. This "talent," which has resulted in the "feminization of work," has both created opportunities for women, and, at the same time, "put to work" the entirety of women's lives. Changing the style and rules of the organization of labor does not mean that the relations of power have been displaced. Indeed, these relations remain intact so long as men hold themselves to be the only beings endowed with *intelligence, will,* and *moral sense* and women are regarded as naturally complementary to men. Making matters worse, the "feminization of work"—a significant cultural shift in which both men and women are implicated—has meant in practice that women alone are responsible for uniting family and work. The demands of combining work and family are, in fact, a collective responsibility rather than the natural destiny of women.

As Pogliana makes clear at the outset, corporations, which treat women as if they were empty containers, have the upper edge. The experiences so generously recounted by Pogliana's subjects, which illustrate women's enormous investment of passion and personal growth at work, ought to have "expand[ed] the gaze of institutional agents," but, alas, they did not. Women continue to perform a tremendous amount of invisible and taken-for-granted labor in the workplace—labor that goes unrecognized and unacknowledged because it's regarded as part of the "female nature." How advantageous to productivity! But to hope for recognition from those perpetrating an injustice is merely to avoid conflict and confrontation. It is more important to expand the gaze of other women in similar situations and to provide them with the collective strength and wisdom needed to effectively change the relations of power.

In the many entangled situations in which women are inappropriately treated as subordinate, regardless of their personal merit and commitment, the absence of conflict is striking. The struggle to hold the conception of themselves as persons and the interests of the firm—work and affect—"harmoniously together" is difficult to sustain. Because of their multiple competencies, flexibility, and adaptability, women are now present in more domains, and they are barely able to conceal the acrobatic and exhausting effort required to simultaneously inhabit traditionally hostile and mutually exclusive domains.

Combining family and work outside the home is frowned upon. Its opponents disapprove of the pleasure, success, and new affective relations that become available to women outside the home. Critics prefer that women dedicate themselves to family and housework; they argue that these commitments constitute an obstacle to women's effectiveness and advancement in the workplace—by, for example, necessitating programs such as maternity leave. But women's awareness grows, despite the effort it requires and the many contradictions that must be unraveled: "Motherhood and the firm are incompatible," insists Pogliana. The role of emotions and an appealing manner (*seduttività*) in the workplace, instead of allowing for the "recognition of what is uniquely feminine, as a value," often becomes ancillary. Positions in which one thinks and decides reside firmly in male hands, whereas women occupy positions that are judged to be more suitably traditional, such as director of personnel and training.

It is noteworthy that while the female "talents," such as listening and mediation, are increasingly exalted publicly, women, despite rivalries, diffidence, and hostility, struggle to advance their careers in solitude. More than the recognition of bosses, husbands, and children, for which, fatally, they wait in a state of insecurity, women need to become aware of the history uniting them and the strength to be gained from collective undertaking.

The analyses and evaluation of the work experiences of older women and women of various social classes oscillate between two poles—on the one hand, they note the advantages and the greater number of competencies that women bring to the economy, and, on the other hand, they observe that women slip into forms of self-exploitation that consume their whole lives and ultimately leave them feeling "prostituted out." Some women seek to unchain themselves from this onerous and complicit position by taking small administrative jobs that offer little satisfaction or affirmation. Others locate their very identity in the firm and in their work, by which they feel affirmed, especially within the professional context.

> The worker is asked to perform a certain form of embodiment, always friendly and smiling. It is possible that this creates a greater feeling of prostituting oneself, because when the work of relationship-building becomes central, one must be prepared to use and exploit the capacities of the body, even to the extent of mimicking sexual advances.... In atypical jobs, the personal and relational component always takes on greater importance, whether in the context of the work itself or in the contractual relations with the boss. One must look good, be desirable. One does not know one's rights, nor even with whom one might discuss them at work.[33]

Pogliana goes further:

> There is a sort of white noise that accompanies women in business, no matter what areas they work in. In order for a woman to be heard, a certain kind of attention is required: a woman is first and foremost a body. One must always refer to her physicality, to her role as a woman before any other role, even before that of being a manager.... When she enters a meeting or takes the podium on stage, every woman knows that she will be judged by her attire, her hair, etc.... One

can say that, even in corporations, the showgirl model of women has taken hold.... Demonstrating one's willingness to be seduced is not only appreciated at the personal level but has also become a sort of unofficial requirement. At the least, it must be considered seriously.[34]

The discussion about women and work, no matter which ideological side it arises from, fails to extract itself from *the equality/difference* binary, which has also contaminated elements of feminism. This failure persists even though feminists have long been aware that this binary presents a false dichotomy imposed upon women by male power. If it was relatively easy for the 1970s generation to distance itself from a male model of emancipation, a process of liberation that must criticize all forms of dualism, as well as the notions of complementarity and the reunification of opposites, will be all the more torturous and uncertain now. It is striking that women, at the moment at which their identity and sense of community are coming undone and being eclipsed, are contesting, whether as revenge or as affirmation of their newfound authority, the idea of a specifically female "nature" or gender—an idea deployed by men in order to confine women to a minority social, legal, and political status.

But women face many incongruencies and contradictions, and those analyses that explicitly seek to valorize gender differences are particularly problematic:

> Think of requests for small services that, for a man in a certain position, would never be made (for example, taking a memo). In this practice lies an attempt to lead the woman back to a "feminine" identity, thereby diminishing her position as a professional, especially when that position is ancillary. Recall that, in terms of work, men expect strategic roles that require thought, whereas women expect executive and organizational roles. We even see (nothing new!) women reduced to their private roles: behaving in a motherly fashion, receiving attention on account of her physical appearance.... Establishing good relations and taking care of people

are ways of responding to often inexplicit needs: for example, serving as a refuge in a conflict, especially in conflicts with one's employees and colleagues. Women experience this problem in work relations (perhaps in all relations): the inability to manage situations of conflict without excessive suffering, without being dragged into endless conversations.[35]

The reconciliation of love, motherhood, and work with the struggle to become a whole person, both in public and in private, continues to be pursued by women, despite relapses into ancillary roles, the extra labor they perform, and the disappointment they encounter. Their determination to have female "authority" recognized in the workplace is met with evasion and avoidance by the men and institutions that wield power. But is it simply the need to be loved and the hope for a shared affection that fixes women to the dream of an integrated and harmonious family? In the changing of women's roles, is it not perhaps the prospect of female omnipotence—accessing public power without renouncing private, seductive, and maternal power—that women unconsciously desire and men fear?

The Mother: The First and Last Taboo

One can only hope for a lively debate, much like the one that played out in French newspapers, following the translation of Elisabeth Badinter's book *Le conflit: La femme et la mère* into Italian.[36] But it is best not to let one's hopes get too high. The interview with the author[37] that appeared in the *Repubblica delle Donne* seems not to have provoked much of reaction. Typically, Ferdinanda Vigliani and Paola Leonardi's collection of interviews with "special women," titled *Perché non abbiamo avuto figli*,[38] went largely unnoticed. Yet women continue to be marginalized in the workplace, and, at the same time, are expected to be excellent mothers and outstanding professionals. These expectations are not new, and the difficulties faced by women are exacerbated by the maternalistic rhetoric that defines female anatomy as destiny.

In 1906, Sibilla Aleramo's autobiography, *Una donna* [*A Woman*],[39] gave voice to the conflict that led her to the "scandalous" decision to leave her husband and child.

> In truth, apart from the amount of energy I used to expend on the baby, I felt increasingly unable to see, to will, to live; it was as if a moral fatigue had superimposed itself on my physical exhaustion. I was unhappy with myself, and my better part chastised myself for what I underwent.... In me, the mother did not integrate with the woman.... I lacked the continuous will of the educator, the serenity of spirit required to guide this small existence. I could not be entirely absorbed by the consideration of its needs; I could not prevent or satisfy them. At certain points, I hated myself for this very awareness. I was so miserable when I failed, even after I accepted the sacrifice of my individuality, forgot myself, to focus all of my energies on that individual that was being formed next to me.[40]

It was assumed that women did not need to affirm their individuality, that they were destined to live for others, to love and give birth. And this self-sacrifice was made into a religion; extolling this sacrifice became the highest tribute that thinkers such as Jules Michelet, Johann Jakob Bachofen, and Paolo Mantegazza could offer to female difference. The latter, for instance, declared: "The woman-mother is the whole woman: the young, beautiful, rich woman cannot be happy if she is not a mother. The woman who is not a mother is the eunuch of her sex. Unfortunately, the intricate mechanism that constitutes our civil society produces thousands of these mutilated women every day."[41]

More provocatively, Carla Lonzi, in *La donna clitoridea e la donna vaginale* [The clitoral woman and the vaginal woman], launched a radical feminism that shook the foundations of traditional roles, challenged the certainties of female identity, and disrupted the equilibrium between nature and history, family and society, individual and collective, all of which had theretofore survived hundreds of years of change.

The patriarchal couple is the couple of the penis and vagina, husband and wife; it is father and mother, procreative animal culture. Their relation was not determined by sex, but by procreation, to which women were subjected. The vaginal woman carries on this culture: She is the woman of patriarchy and the seat of all maternal myths.[42]

Evidently, the separation of sexuality from procreation, the legalization of abortion, the termination of the many violations of freedom that have historically burdened women, including the murder of many women, are insufficient to alter the entrenched notion of the foundation of female identity—that is, motherhood. Just when feminism succeeded in shifting women's place from the home to the public sphere, the dilemma of equality-difference, based on the idea of a hierarchy of complementary genders, returns with a vengeance and in a most uncritical manner. It is no accident that this return is expressed by a feminism committed to "thinking difference"; neither is it by chance that we see new female figures, such as wives and escorts, standing up to powerful men; we also see women, both mothers and workers, as the subject uniquely responsible for holding together all of life in its entirety. From an *aut-aut* [either/or], which constrains women within the bounds of complementarity, women are moving to an *et-et* [and-and], that is, to an ideal union in which the allegedly "divergent natures" of males and females combine in each of us.

If the fundamental parts of the whole self can only be realized through motherhood and a professional life—and not, as one might expect, through the body and thought, a notion of the complete human that men have reserved for themselves—then the motive for thinking difference becomes clear: "When we say yes to motherhood, we give shape to a desire inscribed in our bodies and minds—a desire that, when freely acted upon, carries with it the necessity and the pleasure, even the physical pleasure, of staying close to the child. This is so not only when the child is little, but also intermittently during other phases of growth. Paternity inscribes itself in a different way."[43]

Badinter remains wedded to a logic of opposition by insisting that the only way to escape the fetters of the traditional definition of the female essence is to refuse to have children. Badinter's position has the merit of bringing, once again, the domestic domain to our attention—that crucial locus of the experience that lies at the origin of both sexes, that is, birth. Men have long envied and subjugated the power to give birth by confining it to nature, and women now claim it as a "true and proper gesture of freedom," a power that needs to be recognized and valued. We should not be surprised, then, that some of the younger generation of women do not perceive the difficulties implicit in the "double yes," or that others defiantly proclaim, "No. No to motherhood in these conditions."

> Why must I be a mother? For the sole reason that I'm a woman? There is a taste of the wild in saying no. There is pleasure in saying: Let my hands remain free of chains. I have much to give to the world—more than that needed by only one individual. I need to remain with myself now, in this world. I do not wish to be two only because one must be so. It seems that when the principal occupation of a woman is not that of mother, but of citizen, there is always someone who wants to put her in her place.[44]

Situated between the sacred and the natural, motherhood is the first and last sacred cow of male-dominated culture. Motherhood has the power to divide women, but it also has the power (and why not?) to catalyze a movement capable of extending and deepening the analysis of the relation between the sexes.

Chapter Three

The Circle of Men

Warrior Asceticism

In *L'ultimo paradosso* [The ultimate paradox], Alberto Asor Rosa presented a series of "remarks, notes, observations, and thoughts on the fundamental problems of existence." Contemplating what it means to be a man, he wrote:

> Men: For centuries we have sat around tables—either round or rectangular—as a group, issuing orders and distributing power appropriate to our respective roles. Even among friends we don our protective suits of armor: the most intimate moments of our conversations lie deeply hidden. Our hands are claws at rest. The proud do all of this with dignity and pride, but the lowly parade this behavior in a cowardly way in order to instill fear. Both, however, stand upright; their armor protects their backs and they can lean their tired hips against their swords. Our faces, our bodies lie behind tarnished and blinding spoils. But we dare not renounce our circle and its laws, even should we be promised unlimited freedom and unequaled joy in exchange. We sit and listen to ourselves extol our form, our honor, our heroism and our dignity, our being-for-itself, all safeguarded by a simulacrum of steel and a mask of iron. We are surrounded only by subordinates and buffoons, and among them we place women. We even pretend to like them and find them pleasing, displaying our knightly virtues

for them, which ultimately alienates us even further from them. In our protective armor, we find ourselves somewhat trapped: when we move, the hinges creak and we are in pain. We sometimes suspect that our sacrifice, offered to abstract and cruel divinities like those in the religions of ascetic warriors, is worthless or useless, even pathetic. We may aspire to escape through the cracks in our ancient armor, to slip unseen from the table and through the door in order to breathe fresh air. Through the fissure of our disguise, ... we glimpse our own desperation, our prison, our pain, our exaggerated pride, our contempt for all those outside the circle. But the moment our gaze catches the gaze of our companions, it finds itself enchained; the desire for freedom, the excitement of joy, immediately abandon us. We discover that we can never leave the circle of men.... The only advance we have made in this culture of men in the last two thousand years has been the suppression of monarchy. But this did not negate the circle; rather, it reinforced it by freeing it from the weakest link. Men have been living in this way for centuries, and if they persist in this way, they will founder.[1]

After reading an article in *Liberazione* that featured the views of ten men on the question of why men kill women, I was thinking about Asor Rosa's reflections on men and the destiny of his book, judged by the intellectuals closest to Asor Rosa as belonging in the attic, where it seems to have languished.[2] Two things in the *Liberazione* article never cease to surprise me: first, the power or presumption (*prepotenza*) that disguises itself as neutrality, that is, the habit of men to think of themselves as prototypical of the human race; and, second, the suddenness with which this arrogance and presumption seem able to disappear, as if they are masks that can easily and rapidly be donned and discarded. The male domination that permeates both private and public spheres and the awareness of the violence perpetrated against women by patriarchy are treated as undeniable cultural and experiential truths in newspaper articles. These analyses have always presented, albeit in different forms, a general political engagement.

If women struggled, amid intrigue and numerous obstacles, to develop an awareness of their oppression—an allegedly fragile awareness that threatens to disappear after every gain—it is men, apparently, who, reasoning about a representation of the world produced by a male version of history, are better able to bring sexism to light, to illuminate the logic of love and violence that sustains it. Why, one wonders, this extreme defense of a stubborn, unconvincing neutrality, which expresses itself in a political analysis that negates the relation between the sexes, obscuring and distorting the relation between the sexes' localization in social questions such as the marginalization, incomplete citizenship, and economic exploitation of women?

It seems that women must struggle "to know" how deeply they've been oppressed, how distant they remain from the goal of being and being perceived as whole individuals, as unities of body and thought, to know that they settled for an emancipation that conceives them in the same terms that were used to justify their oppression: body, sexuality, maternity. Even the daily violence they experience—the fruit of fear and intimidation, the leading cause of the deaths of women—remains invisible, and this invisibility is maintained by the desires and fantasies of love.

The presumption that men "know" is evidence of the privilege accorded to them by history and the necessity of their alleged "destiny." Though this evidence is rarely identified as privilege, it must be clearly named as such if women are to be freed from blame for their own oppression.

The historical community of men has witnessed the collapse of empires, borders, and walls, and has overcome intractable hatreds, yet men are reluctant to let the fragile wall—no stronger than the front doors of their houses—that separates their public image of "virility" from their experience as sons, fathers, husbands, and lovers—crumble.

But all that remains unspoken in history eventually forms an entire galaxy of willful ignorance, which men fill with goods. They cling to their secret by looking backward, confusing hope with nostalgia, and the female body, irrefutably seen as a possession, becomes, in the male imagination, a fertile, uncontaminated land capable of constantly being reborn.

For centuries, generations of men have transmitted, from fathers to sons, the same sense of community across all domains—from home, to work, to play. Men have been sure to legitimate their entrances and departures from one domain to another with a freedom that accords with their "natural" privilege. This privilege, which is daily and enduringly manifested in the relations between men and women, is an infinitesimal kind of violence that never reaches the front pages of the newspaper. Indeed, it is so small that one does not bother to trace it, even when it escalates to blows and then to knives. In an epoch in which the authority of fathers, by reason of natural decrepitude or the inevitable discontinuity produced by changing awareness, is beginning to decline, and passion seems to be losing its force, men increasingly seem to draw vigor only from violence.

As the numbers of male models of social authority decrease, as the legitimacy of institutions whose neutrality masks the sediment of old distinctions, values, hierarchies, and privilege declines, the myths of force and honor begin to decay; it is as if the terrain—the land in which children were wrenched from their mothers in order to forge courageous warriors—has dried up. This violent rupture, much like the scission that separates and differentiates the male from the female body that gives it life, has served as a form of initiation to a training that inculcates fidelity to new codes of belonging, which facilitate the move from family to a social community, such as, for example, the military or the church.

The script of masculinity, destined to repeat itself without variation through the course of life, used to be everywhere and always confirmed by respected thinkers and family members alike and in the behavior of parental figures, whose roles were rigidified by obligation, duty, domestic rituals, and the traditional distribution of power, all of which were consonant with the structures of public life. Patriarchal rule, whether that of patrician or farmer, even when rendered uglier by alcoholism, never failed to secure some degree of obedience and respect. Violence was confused with law, tradition, and behavioral norms with a power that was considered "natural." Without such conformity, itself made of flesh and passion, no social order would have been able to endure for so long, to withstand the discontinuities of history or to resist the assault by new generations.

When women began to move beyond the places to which they had been consigned—spaces either vilified or exalted—those spaces theretofore designated as male began to lose their defined and indisputable borders. Freedom, which the historical male community, unchained from the primary, material conditions of survival, believed was theirs to enjoy, ruthlessly demonstrated its fickleness in bringing to light a hinterland inhabited by fragility, fears, and insecurities.

The Armed Defenselessness of the Man-Son

The domination of women by men is distinguished from all other historical relations of power by its profound and contradictory implications: first, the *confusion* of *love* with *violence*. We encounter here a domination that arises out of the intimate relations of sex and motherhood. Many prefer not to recognize the most ancient and enduring relation between love and hate, tenderness and rage, life and death—a relation expressed in the claims that one must destroy in order to preserve, that one kills out of excessive love, that one's group, nation, or culture is superior to, even the enemy of, another's.

In *Civilization and Its Discontents* (1929), Freud, having identified eros and thanatos, love and death, as originary drives, was compelled to admit that they are less polarized than it might initially seem. The intersection between them is particularly surprising in the relation between a person and his or her love object.

> The element of truth behind all this, which people are so ready to disavow, is that men are not gentle creatures who want to be loved, and who at the most can defend themselves if they are attacked; they are, on the contrary, creatures among whose instinctual endowments is to be reckoned a powerful share of aggressiveness. As a result, their neighbour is for them not only a potential helper or sexual object, but

also someone who tempts them to satisfy their aggressiveness on him, to exploit his capacity for work without compensation, to use him sexually without his consent, to seize his possessions, to humiliate him, to cause him pain, to torture and to kill him.[3]

Rather than demanding harsher penalties for aggressors or better safeguards for victims, it might make more sense to examine those areas of personal life that have to do with our most intimate feelings and all that is most familiar to us—those areas in which we would most like to eradicate violence. The murder, rape, and physical and psychological abuse of women are widely documented and discussed in the daily newspapers; these horrific acts, especially when particularly cruel or spectacular, are featured on their front pages. The violation, abuse, and killing of women are largely carried out by husbands, sons, fathers, and lovers who are incapable of tolerating the walls of domestic life, walls that excessively, or in some cases do not, protect women. Equally intolerable is the embrace and/or abandonment that exposes unexpected male fragility.

Few seem to be troubled by the fact that the body most persecuted by men is the same body that gave them life, the body that first provided them with nourishment and sexual stimulation—a body that men find again in their adult lives and through which they dream of reliving the intimate and originary experience of belonging to another. This body, which could bestow life or death, love or abandonment, cared for the male when he was most dependent and helpless. Confining women to the role of mother—caretaker of the home, children, and sex—men have positioned themselves as the eternal child and thus forced themselves to wear the unstable mask of masculinity in perpetuity. The *flight from the feminine*, which underlies and reinforces the historical community of men, is also a flight from infantile needs that are rooted in a timeless immobility.

The family prolongs infancy and constructs indispensable ties of reciprocity between mother and child while arming the hand that will breach them. We all—both men and women—seek shelter from an increasingly conflictual society by taking refuge in and thus preserving the institutions and ideas of the most enduring and enigmatic domination in history: the undeclared war that leads men, motivated by ancient fears and desires, to celebrate their triumph over the female body, with which men were once united and to which they confusedly return in a loving embrace. If men were actually self-assured, natural "winners," they would not need to humiliate and kill. By restricting women to the role of mother, patriarchy permits women to extend their material and psychological power over their children, especially their male children, beyond infancy. This power, which comes from making oneself indispensable to another, has now become, for women, one of the greatest obstacles to their ability to realize themselves as complete individuals, to become citizens in the fullest sense of the term.

Another contradiction, linked to the first, is also rooted in childhood. Before becoming possessive husbands and fathers, before becoming authoritarian and violent, men, born of women, are treasured children. It is tempting to blame society for the transformation of the male from loving son to violent man—a transition that segues smoothly into the exercise of power by the community of men. Certainly, it is more reassuring than thinking that ambivalent feelings are an ineluctable aspect of intimate relations.

In *Three Guineas*, Virginia Woolf observed:

> Inevitably, we look upon societies as conspiracies that sink the private brother, whom many of us have reason to respect, and inflate in his stead a monstrous male, loud of voice, hard of fist, childishly intent upon scoring the floor of the earth with chalk marks, within whose mystic boundaries human beings are penned. Decorated like a savage with feathers, he goes through mystic rites and enjoys the dubious pleasure of power and dominion while we, "his" women, are locked in the private house without share in the many societies of which his society is composed.[4]

But noting that the public and private worlds are "inseparably connected," Woolf concluded that the "tyrannies and slavery of one are the tyrannies and slavery of the other."

The first great revolution in the analysis of sexism in Italy was made by the women's movement of the 1970s, which shifted attention from the public sphere to personal life, from the "female question"—that is, issues of social disadvantage and questions of legal and political status, in terms of which women were regarded and treated as a minority like any other—to relations between the sexes. In Italy, the struggle for women's emancipation, originally framed in terms of achieving equal rights—that is, full citizenship, understood as parity with men, and the valorization of women's "domestic talents" (the "virtues of the heart," to borrow an expression from Maria Montessori)—shifted to the demand for an end to patriarchy and an analysis of male domination, understood as the expropriation of female existence itself: the identification of women with the body, the objectification and commodification of women, the conflation of sexuality with maternity, the circumscription of female sexuality to obligatory reproductive services.

Although feminists do not address the "enigma of origins"—the process of differentiation that opposes, hierarchizes, and renders complementary male and female, thought and body, history and biology—feminist theory and practice are predicated on the *dualism of the sexes*—the historical definitions of femininity and masculinity, the sexual division of roles and work—which situates men as protagonists in public life and relegates women, dedicated to the protection of family interests and the preservation of life, to the home. It is not surprising that, at the moment women became conscious of having internalized a male vision of the world, they were inclined to seek their autonomy in the domains of thinking and feeling: the experience of their own bodies, the discovery and legitimation of their own sexuality as distinct from procreation, the determination of whether to carry a pregnancy to term. These were the central themes of consciousness-raising groups, which sought to explore the unconscious and saw in psychoanalysis an essential kind of knowing that could avoid lapsing into ideology. Marxist and workers' groups such as Lotta Femminista brought another perspective to the women's movement, analyzing motherhood, child care, and the maintenance of the family in terms of the production and reproduction of the workforce—unpaid labor performed in the name of love and directly benefiting the economy in general and capital in particular.

In both cases, what remained unexplored was the ambiguous, contradictory relation between the sexes that we call *love*: the love between mother and child as well as that between man and woman. Certainly, much has been said about the relations between mothers and daughters and those between women, but the discussion was always framed in terms of sexuality, homosexuality, and lesbianism.

In *Masculine Domination*, Pierre Bourdieu, twenty years after the feminist movement, refocused attention on "symbolic violence"—the internalization of particular concepts and attitudes, a mental habitus that leads victims to speak the same language as that of their aggressors. Bourdieu concluded the book with a "postscript on domination and love" in which he raised a troubling doubt: He suggested that "the enchanting universe of love relations" is the sole, though significant, exception to the laws of male domination," that love constitutes a "miraculous truce" that makes reciprocity between the sexes possible. In this formulation, losing oneself in another at the expense of oneself in a state of perfect fusion, beyond egoism and altruism, is also possible. But might it not be the case that love is considered the "highest" relation only because it is the "most subtle, the most invisible" form of symbolic violence?[5]

Love is surely the experience in which it is most difficult to trace the border between the destinies of man and woman, the experience in which the creator, "different than an egocentric and dominating Pygmalion," lives as "the creature of his creature." Perfect moments of passion occur in the binary relation of love, but here one also finds that positions and roles are continually exchanged: possessing and being possessed, conquering and being conquered, procreation and birth. Perhaps it was not possible to restore and reclaim women's sexuality without freeing it from the chains of motherhood and love, for the sake of which women often renounced their own desires. Perhaps a radical break—a provocative gesture, such as Carla Lonzi's *Sputiamo su Hegel* [Let's spit on Hegel], published by Rivolta Femminile in the early 1970s—was necessary:

> The female sex is the clitoris, the male sex is the penis.... In men, the mechanism of pleasure is strictly connected to reproduction, whereas in women, the mechanisms of pleasure and reproduction communicate with one another but do not coincide.[6]

When Lonzi described the "vaginal woman" as "colonized," she was referring to the age-old submission of women to the pleasure of men, a submission often compelled by means of violence. But she obscures the fact that the penetration of the female by the male genitals, which does not result in orgasm for most women, runs counter to fantasies and desires linked to the primordial form of love—the singular unrepeatable *unity of two* that are mother and child before and immediately following birth. We might hypothesize that love is a fantasy, which continues into adulthood, about the period between *coitus* and *birth*; it reappears in the relationship of a couple as eros, the essence of which Freud described as the making of oneself into "more than one." Men, who were once helpless children, come to occupy the position of dominance that their mothers once occupied vis-à-vis them, at the same time that they struggle to conquer the trauma of birth and their early experience of fragility and dependence.

In coitus, the desire to lose oneself in the indistinctness of the body from which one was generated, as well as the desire to flee from the danger of again being absorbed by that body, are intertwined and confused with one another. Even leaving rage aside, there is a violent aspect to the penetrative character of male genital sexuality, and this implicit violence is related to deep-seated fears—fears that also limit men. The female body encountered in adult relations of love cannot but reactivate the originary experience of the mother's body, evoking both the tenderness of fusion and the fear of the loss of one's autonomy, feelings of fragility, impotence, and of being overwhelmed. Of course, an ideology that identifies all women as mothers and consequently continues to infantilize men reinforces this retention of this early body memory.

The dominance of men, husbands, and fathers thus arises not only as a historical construction meant to safeguard the male-son from his early experience of helplessness, but also, as Stefano Ciccone, in *Essere maschi* [Being males], maintains, from his *marginalization* in the reproductive process.

> I refer, first, to an asymmetry between the two sexes that is *perceived* as a check on the male body—that it appears as an accessory to the reproductive process, which the history of men has displaced with symbolic constructions and networks of power that occlude the foundation of human continuity; men have forged this construction and they continue to enforce it. Standing before two *different* bodies, men have not attempted to make sense of their own being in the world in terms of their own bodies; rather, they have constructed roles, powers, and narratives that almost erase their relative lack of importance in the reproductive process and, at the same time, assert the centrality of men. I am thinking here of the need to control women's bodies, . . . to devalue corporeity (perceived as female domain) and thereby reduce it to an instrument of a disincarnate subject that believes itself to be free of its chains.[7]

In the male imaginary, birth and coitus become confused with one another. This confusion, which underlies notions of the secondary and subservient nature of women, can be traced in Johann Jakob Bachofen's mythology of origins and in Jules Michelet's romantic infantilization of women. According to Bachofen,

> Women precede and men follow; women come first. Men stand in a filial relation to women. The woman *is*, men are born from her as her first fruit. . . . Within the domain of physical existence, the male principle occupies a secondary place, it is subordinated to the female principle. . . . This is why the son becomes the husband, the fertilizer of the mother, the father. . . . From the start, he will become the fertilizer of the mother; from the moment of his generation, he is himself a generator. In front of him, there is always the same woman, both mother and spouse. The son becomes his own father.[8]

The main characters at the beginning of the story—mother and son—reappear at the story's end, but their positions are reversed. The horizontal line of historical becoming is transformed into a circle by an instantaneous short circuit that fuses together *beginning* and *end*, *origin* and *history*, *mother* and *son*, *woman* and *man*. Passing in rapid succession, the figures of son, fertilizer, and father are experienced as one and the same; the male figure has arrogated for himself all creative powers as well as the omnipotence that he once ascribed to his mother. Coitus adopts the form of birth and, in turn, gives form to it. It is a *taking possession* in reverse that signals the closure of the circle. In this overturning in which the male takes the place of mother, female existence, which consigns itself over to men and expects regeneration from them, is seen, and not by sheer chance, as a male child.

In Michelet's romantic idealization of love, understood as the dream of fusion, it is more difficult to undo the knot of love and domination.

> Nature privileges men. It gives women to men as weak and in love, dependent in their need to be loved and protected. Nature, on account of its innocent daughter, defers to the magnanimity of men, and men, who make the laws, become privileged. They arm themselves against a weak, suffering creature....
>
> ... The task of women is to remake the hearts of men. Protected, supported by them, women support men with love. Love is women's work....
>
> ... Man, who is older than woman, dominates his companion by virtue of experience, and loves her like a daughter.... But when his labor and exertion render man stopped with fatigue, woman, sober and serious, the true genius of the home, ministers to him like a mother....
>
> ... The woman enters wholly and forever into the union. She desires to be reborn together with and by means of man. One needs to understand her words, remake her, renew her, create her.... A man intuits that a woman will love him even more if she is made his and the same as him. Take her, then, as she is given, into your heart and arms; receive her as a tender child.[9]

The exchange of parts between the weak and the strong, the dominated and the dominator, produces a deceptive appearance of reciprocity, behind which the patriarchal order that subjugates women to the interests and well-being of men is evident. If to the eyes of the man-son the mother is the powerful body that generated, cared for, and holds him still in her arms, for the man-husband (the father whose historical triumph depends on his disavowal of his biological roots), the woman, always being mother, even when the companion of men, is expected to "regenerate him," physically and morally, from the fatigue of work; she must support and comfort him in his social efforts. Furthermore, she must transfer all of her energies to him, sacrifice her own life in order to "become one with him."

Both Michelet and Bachofen see woman solely as mother and child. Neither can conceive of a woman as a female individual. Even when it is admitted that women have a soul, it is argued that their souls must be nourished by the ideas and guidance of men; women must be completely penetrated by a man's love in order to be one with him.

In the double nature of woman—"weak and in love, dependent," needing to be loved and protected, but also maternally devoted to the care and service of men—the historical servitude of women, along with their exaltation in the male imagination, are grounded in a contradictory fashion. But most important is the fact that behind a domination rendered imperceptible by the fable of love, the weakness and fragility of men disappear.

The connection between helplessness, dependency, and domination in the male experience is made explicit in an essay by Sándor Ferenczi, titled *Thalassa* (1924):

> Humans are dominated by a regressive tendency that aims to reestablish the intrauterine situation.... Toward the end of the development of the libido, the child returns to its primitive object, the mother. This time, however, the child is armed with a weapon. The erect penis is perfectly able to find the path to the maternal vagina; it is completely adept at finding its way....

> ... Evolution, including coitus, cannot have any other end than the attempt of the I, which is truly uncertain and ineffective, even though it is presented as being defined and somewhat successful, to return to the mother's body—a situation prior to the extremely painful break between the I and the external world. This temporary regression can be achieved in three ways: (a) through hallucinations and dreams, during sleep; (2) by symbolically acting out the I's return to the mother's body; and (3) by means of ejaculation, insofar as sperm, the representative of the I and its narcissistic double, the genital organ, has the privilege of actually penetrating the interior of the maternal body....
>
> ... These observations ... lead us to think that coitus is also a repetition, at the individual level, of the struggle between the sexes. Woman is on the losing side of the battle: ceding to man the privilege of penetrating the maternal body, she must content herself with compensatory fantasies, and, above all, by welcoming the child with whom she shares her happiness.[10]

Besides offering pleasure, coitus satisfies two opposing tendencies:

> The increase of painful tension and its culmination in orgasmic satisfaction represent the repetition of the painful experience of birth and its felicitous result, as well as the reestablishment of the intrauterine situation of perfect well-being, obtained by penetrating the womb: ... a commemorative festival that celebrates the happy liberation from a difficult situation....
>
> ... Surviving the danger inherent in birth and discovering the joy of existence outside the maternal body are, for human beings, undeniable experiences, from which arises the pursuit of periodic and analogous situations of danger, however small, the only aim of which is to enjoy their being overcome.[11]

The war between the sexes, in which, according to Ferenczi, men are the victims, plays out around birth and coupling, through which the general biological tendency that "compels living beings to seek to return to the state of tranquillity they enjoyed prior to their births" is manifested.

Unable to deny that both sexes desire to return to the womb, Ferenczi argues that women experience "passive pleasure" during the sexual act, that is, a pleasure produced by an imaginary identification with the triumphant male—the possessor of the penis—and, above all, with the child, during intercourse.

> On the erotic plane, she is similar to the child, who wants to be loved and who tenaciously and voluntarily holds on to the fantasy of still being wholly inside the mother's body. In this way, she can easily identify with the fetus that lives in her (or with the penis that is its symbol).[12]

We also find here echoes of Freud's reading of female sexuality: If men take those who feed, care for, and protect the child—"that is, the mother or the one who fulfills the same functions as the mother"—as their sexual object, then, for women, the child itself becomes "a sexual object in the full sense of the term." According to Freud, this process is so powerful that a marriage can be considered successful when the wife relates to her husband as her son.

Whatever the perspective, whether Michelet's romantic idealism or Ferenczi's bio-analysis, the dynamic that underpins male domination follows the same trajectory: In order to guarantee its return, even if only imaginary, to the originary beatitude of the unity of two, to the continuity of maternal care, woman must remain mother, stripped of her sexual power and her own identity and purpose, and come to identify with a man and take upon herself the fragility and helplessness that once belonged to the son.

In one of his last letters to his mother before he committed suicide at the tender age of twenty-three, Carlo Michelstaedter wrote: "It seems to me that you were never outside of me; rather, we continued to be one person . . . just like we were twenty-one years and five months ago. And this is basically the relation between mother and son as defined by nature. A mother is the only person capable of loving in this way, never needing to affirm her individuality and without this being a sacrifice."[13]

It is important that the woman be disposed toward self-sacrifice in order for the individuality of the son to flourish, as Rousseau instructed in *Émile*: "Raise them from infancy, care for them when they are grown, advise and console them, make their lives pleasurable and sweet." Her dedication is even more stalwart when the mother succeeds at "becoming her son," when she lives only through him, his work, his success in the world.

In order to fully enjoy his autonomy, his freedom in the public sphere, a man must annihilate the biological chains of his birth from a female body and of all that bodies represent for him: fragility, mortality, his early dependency on his mother. Although men exalt women in their imaginations, they have projected their own weakness, guilt, and all that belongs to the heritage of our animal nature, including our limits as living beings, onto women. In order to degrade maternal and erotic power, man has forced woman to live a reflexive life, to embody and become her fears and desires, to be simultaneously glorified and subjugated.

In debasing the bodies of women, man has also debased his own body along with the passions that course through it. Through the image that men have forged of the other sex, they have erected an internal conflict between *helplessness and power*, between dependency on and annihilation of all connections, between embodiment and thought, feeling and reason.

As Luce Irigaray so elegantly put it,

> You searched and searched for me, in you. Wanting me still to be virgin material for the building of your world to come. (10)
>
> The skin of a living being. I was your house. And, when you leave, abandoning this dwelling place, I do not know what to do with these walls of mine. Have I ever had a body other than the one which you constructed according to your idea of it? Have I ever experienced a skin other than the one which you wanted me to dwell within? (49)
>
> You made me powerful to let me pay you back—to the nth degree. Good earth, good breeder. And good wife too.... I participate in your subject.... You never meet me except as your creature—within the horizon of your world. (45–47)

> Inherent in your horizon is the function to which you have reduced me. The matter and the tool which I remain to build your dwelling place. (48)
>
> That abyss which you create by having always already made it disappear inside you. Inside you—so that you can exist. You have assimilated it: to be. And it makes a hole in your horizon. She, who became you, is missing. (54)[14]

Men have armed themselves in order not to see their weakness; they have made the silence of their bodies the condition for a subjectivity free of chains, for governing and having power. As Ciccone has observed, men have distanced themselves not only from their mothers, but from themselves. By breaking with embodiment per se, they have rendered themselves "amputated, strangers to [their] very own bodies."[15]

The broadening of female liberty and autonomy, even though it exposes the inability of men to relate to women as subjects, as individuals and persons, can also serve, according to Ciccone, as "a resource that offers men a different experience of themselves and their own bodies, thereby providing a route of escape from violence."

The Freedom to Be

Of the many meanings of "freedom," two, in particular, are relevant to our discussion: (1) in the negative sense of escape, to flee someone or something, and (2) in the public sense of personhood. "Free," according to Greek and Latin dictionaries, means to not be a slave—that is, to be an adult male belonging to a community of equals charged with governing the city, a son of free parents, endowed with political power and capable of defending himself.

This is the definition of the citizen-warrior. Those outside the terms of this definition and within the domesticity excluded in this understanding of liberty and politics included slaves, women, and adolescents, none of whom were permitted to participate in the public realm and whose lives were expropriated from them. But also sacrificed on the altar of the polis was the individual, whose most personal choices were wholly subjected to the authority of the social body.

A common destiny, then, belongs to the originary relation between freedom and politics: a tear, an act of negation, the need to dislocate oneself from a matrix of chains more or less declared. In the apparent emptiness that lies beyond the world of men are women, bodies, personhood, and parental relations, and the inevitable vicissitudes of every being. Even when highly articulated or extended, freedoms—be they political or individual—remain largely formal; they can easily disappear or be appropriated by one side or another.

Tocqueville's observations about western democracies revealed a paradox: Commenting on the atomization of American society, he noted that "every citizen isolates himself from the masses of his peers; the individual is separated from his family and friends insofar as, after creating a small society for his own use, he willingly abandons larger society." At the same time, however, the individual remains a prisoner of public opinion, which "embraces, guides, and oppresses" him. Less paradoxical than it first seems, the dichotomous phenomena of individualism and uniformity, of political apathy and the increasing power of society over the individual, are but two faces of the same coin, joined in opposition, destined to contradict and devour one another.

In *The Liberty of the Ancients Compared with That of the Moderns* (1819),[16] Benjamin Constant argued that such oppositions are only apparent. The ancient citizen "lived and repeatedly took pleasure" in the exercise of sovereignty and in the "happiness of other individuals," in the "peaceful enjoyment of private independence." These great pleasures of the moderns, however, depended upon the reciprocal support of women whose complementariness was necessary to a dichotomized vision of the citizen—a male vision.

A very long journey was necessary before the conditions and relations given as "natural"—the passions of the body, property, economic inequalities, the sexual division of labor, the drives of love and hate—could emerge from the shadows of public life. But when they did so, their ramifications, even if sometimes elusive, pointed to the very roots of freedom itself, understood as liberation—that is, as "freedom from" some obstacle or hindrance. The historical enigmas of sex, war, exploitation, and dualism belong to the hinterland of freedom; the unspeakable things of history seethe and simmer in the wake of history, disregarded by history itself and limiting its gaze.

Today, we know how small the distance between democracy and totalitarianism is, we understand how easily the biological substrate can become, as it did in the case of Nazism, the "ultimate truth" of the history of a people. We know that war can be mistaken for the defense of life and, hence, for peace; we understand the ambiguous relation between our need for security and protection and our willingness to exchange freedom for (an illusory) safety. At the same time, we cannot ignore the fact that women have been compensated for their subjection by men with secondary and enduring, if illusory, rewards. However, not even the wisdom we've gained seems able to abrade the centuries-old sediment of coercion upon which a fragile freedom—rights destined to remain entirely on paper, "equal" opportunities, and rhetorical equality—is based.

Yet, not long ago, a peaceful revolution began to unfold. Though not without suffering and conflict, this revolution seems to be capable of launching another history, another politics, other forms of living together, other relations between peoples and between the individual and society.

Feminism and other nonauthoritarian movements of the 1970s, by displacing the center of theoretical and political practices from their habitual institutional seats to the body, sexuality, infancy, and the male-female relation, have restored this knowledge and thereby made possible the transformation of those essential human experiences that, having been misrepresented as "natural," were considered unchangeable. Personhood, sex, the unconscious, and primary parental relations, regarded as strange and unspeakable by social theory, are revealed as inextricable components of the idea of freedom once they are no longer seen as "naturally given." Patriarchal freedom is a primary source of contradictions; it is also the source of the erasure of women's being.

If we persist in the notion that human beings are, by nature, either good or evil, it may be because we find it difficult to fix our gaze upon the uncertain region of bio-social-psychology, preferring the relative simplicity of highly specialized fields of inquiry. It is from this region that feminism and other nonauthoritarian movements launched a Copernican revolution; they were secure in their knowledge of the supposed moorings of civilization that had helped to build and nourish a society stubbornly resistant to change.

Writing about L'Asilo di Porta Ticinese, a cooperatively managed daycare in Milan in the early 1970s, Elvio Fachinelli observed:

> It is as if we find ourselves in a violent society, a society in which the strongest and most powerful protect their own families, caught between the fascist and the mafioso.... We see the emergence of a fortified hierarchy, based on strength and power, which stamps itself on the relations between children.... Many children arrive at the kindergarten, at the mere age of three, stiff and restrained—one has the impression that something once available has become frozen. One often has to deal with rigid behaviors, which tend to repeat themselves and which force the adult to assume a coercive role like that adopted by parents, which undoubtedly lies at the root of such behavior.... The childcare worker thus runs the risk of reproducing and reinforcing the child's early experience. In order to attempt to manage these paralyzed children—and I say "attempt"!—it is essential that a *different* adult present itself to the child.... Here, a politics with a *minimum* liberatory sense is required; although it might seem almost impossible, a *radical* politics, understood in the Marxian sense of "taking human beings by their roots," is necessary. An official representative of the Milan Department of Education recently said to me, "Following you requires constructing homes in a different manner; we would need to change the city." This, I think, is what is truly at stake in our project.[17]

The "paradox of repetition," which compels the individual to reenact his or her most meaningful experiences from the period of his or her greatest dependency upon others, is, in Fachinelli's innovative analysis, both an obstacle to and the propellant of freedom; it can manifest as a blind repetition of what has come before or it can serve as the conduit to new forms and behaviors. The return to subservience to a paternal authority that seemed to be in decline, evident in Italy's election of Silvio Berlusconi and bolstered by the dynamics of a consumer society as well as a maternal fantasy, appears as a threat to women. This return inevitably distorts our conception of what is real and what is possible, of our needs and desires, of the relation between the individual and the collective.

But freedom was most radically rethought by feminism, by a consciousness that extracted from a desiccated notion of "naturalness" the most ancient relation of domination, which reserved for the male sex not only the power to determine the fate of the world, but thought itself, the ideational and imaginative constructions that sustain this very relation of domination. The intelligence of men, who have arrogated for themselves alone the prerogatives of human being, was unable, however, to render the process of individuation—that is, the exit from the shared condition of animality—neutral; men, too, are mutilated by that embodied and sexed belonging. Brought into the narrative of personal history through consciousness-raising and self-awareness, non-freedoms (*illibertà*) were newly unveiled. These non-freedoms were not exclusively social, and neither did they all possess the same qualities or express themselves in the same way.

With respect to coercion and the manifest forms of violence that accompany male domination, the "alienation of the I" appears "immense" because this violence is normalized by a representation of the world that is unconsciously transmitted from one generation to the next.

In the Radio 3 interviews by Rossana Rossanda on the "words of politics," Paola Redaelli described the concept of freedom in the following way:

> Freedom is a beautiful word. For me, it means, above all, the freedom to be, the freedom to be different. This is why it is contradictory to equality; it is the freedom to be different despite the laws, beyond the laws, even beyond what are called "the laws of nature." Freedom means being able to choose without negating anything of oneself,

without negating one's intellectual being, one's material needs, one's own deep I. Freedom is the ability to not neglect any part of oneself. It is to transform one's relation with the world to the maximum and without turning back.[18]

A freedom that begins from within by probing lives as they are actually lived, by reaching into the memory of the body, has no limits. Feminism, which opened up this new horizon, is the longest revolution to champion the ultimate frontiers of thought and to incorporate and interrogate the experiences of the body. Sustaining the public's attention requires a secure anchoring in feminist history and culture and a commitment to feminist theory and practice, which, for reasons of haste or fear, were too quickly abandoned. Above all, in order to engage in a genuine dialogue about "female freedom," we must never forget that both the dominated and the dominators have, for millennia, shared the same language, that the alienation of the one comes at the cost of the humanity of the other. Life and politics, now more intertwined than ever, must no longer be understood as the two terms of a false dialectic that abstractly opposes them to one another. Necessity is increasingly propelling life and politics toward perverse ideals or structures—toward the unsuspected relation between the dream of love and biopolitics, between the nostalgia for the unity of mother and child and the search for compact, homogeneous, and uncontaminated social bodies (evident in all forms of nationalism, as well as in ethnic and identitarian uprisings and the contemporary "clash of civilizations"). As for the "sole protagonist of history," who, by means of a sort of doubling, created artificial, false "differences" between the sexes, thus obscuring their real similarities and differences, he must now discover his own face, his own body, his own sex, his own history.

Chapter Four

The Disquieting Slumber of the West

Night Trams

Night trams speak languages both strange and familiar. Often it is the very sounds and intonations of an incomprehensible language that trace the lines of a landscape that gathers us together with other human beings, beyond the differences between our respective cultures and affiliations.

Immigrant workers, who, day in and day out, move invisibly throughout the city as businesses close for the day, are exhaled as a colorful vapor from the mouths of subways. Transportation networks are transformed into a vast domicile for the displaced people of the world. If we overlook the so-called threat presumably posed by every foreigner on the horizon, memory helps us recognize, behind differences of skin or eye color, the figures of a family.

The city makes us free but also inattentive. The city's most recent arrivals inevitably relive memories of a homeland, a countryside, a family, all of which have, as it were, dropped out of time on account of too much pain or unbearable longing. Diverse and multiple voices can finally speak without fear, secure in the indifference of the surrounding passengers; the echoes of pain, travails, and hope that pervade the history of individuals and peoples can be heard in this polyphony. Here, the story of the small death and rebirth that characterizes the abandonment of the place in which one grew up can be heard. Here, anguish and humiliation, as well as the joy of unexpected encounters, can be heard.

Warring worlds—the North and the South, the city and the country—suspended between end-of-day fatigue and the time of rest, inadvertently discover that they share feelings, that their bodies are marked by the same wounds, and that they speak the same language.

Today, xenophobia threatens all forms of living together and makes each day more difficult; the possibility of a shared life is hindered by increasing social inequality and by the fear of and hostility between different cultures. The more tightly we feel the bonds of our mutual need for one another and the greater our intimacy with the bodies of the sick and elderly, the larger looms the figure of the "intruder," ambiguously placed between death and our own survival. The temptation to sever, with one clean cut, the "we" from the "you" (*voi*) appeals to a collectivity that feels threatened by the approach of the distant, that fears familiarization with the foreign and the erosion of the precise confines of its borders.

By annihilating the ground upon which human beings are able to recognize one another as both similar and different, the phantom of the "enemy" not only disturbs the sleep of the West but risks making of history and memory a desert.

Belonging

Is it ever possible to respond to the question "Who are we?" without referring to our belonging—to a sex, a linguistic tradition, a nation, and so on? Can we say "who we are" without saying "who we are not" and "who we are against"?[1] This is the question raised by Samuel P. Huntington about the new world order, which, since the end of the Cold War, has shifted from a rivalry between superpowers to a conflict between civilizations, that is, between cultures and ways of life, between peoples as well as between the people of a single nation—between "us" and "them."

In the face of the decline of the great political ideologies, human beings are increasingly defining themselves in terms of those "things most significant to them": their children, religion, language, history, values, customs, and institutions. Religious symbols such as the crucifix and the Islamic veil, the crusade-like speech surrounding the intervention of western armies in Afghanistan and Iraq, the hot debate about the Christian roots of the nascent European Union—all seem to justify a renewed interest in religion. But we should be suspicious of a return to the most archaic forms of belonging, a return that occurs precisely at the moment in which a destructive and cataclysmic "liquid modernity" seems to create "zombie-like institutions" that, though dead, are maintained by extraordinary measures in order to avert the danger of total collapse.

How can one hypothesize about the coming-to-be of the first and most mysterious "contamination," namely, being two-in-one in the body of the mother, which human beings know in the moment of their birth? The exaggerated need to differentiate oneself becomes violent each time one is confronted with the possibility of absorption or assimilation. The prospect of a mass of individuals worried about utility, insofar as they have been educated to seek utility, produces the specter of an intolerable split between freedom, which today is realized in the life of the individual, and the fear of anonymity.

And in this zone of instability, traditional loci of identification such as the family and the ethnic group install themselves as the anchors of salvation at the same time that we wish to abandon them. Against the loss of borders and flags, which serve to distinguish peoples by means other than their behavior as consumers, the "drive toward connection inevitably reemerges in extreme and violent forms."[2] Ethnic groups, religious communities, nations, and political groups carve out their uniqueness according to "hostile and exclusive" parameters, a move not so different from that employed by men in order to distinguish themselves from women and thereby render them "non-men"—menacing strangers, barbarians.

The need to identify with others and to belong is a primary, originary need that is rooted in the nostalgia for a warm and safe place, which is how our prenatal dwelling is configured in human memory. Paradoxically, this need is linked to the body to which one once intimately belonged, almost without distinction, the body banished and excluded by the historical society of men because it carried with it a frightening difference. It is as if all of the successive relations that humanity created in order to guarantee its survival carried with them that initial offensive and defensive exclusion of women.

The family, including women, sexuality, and all that constitutes our interior, intimate lives, and considered the first building block of social life, has endured a long exile. The domination that history imposed and then claimed as heritage, the subjection of one segment of the population by another in order to exploit it, is the dis-ease that, according to Freud, has afflicted society throughout its continual transformation. Through the centuries, other forms of aggregation, sustained by real or imaginary chains of family ties, similarities, affinities, or shared interests, affirmed differences on the basis of analogous oppositions: internal/external, friend/enemy, good/evil, civilized/barbaric, and so on. Today, in the face of a hitherto unknown social mobility characterized by increasingly fluid relations, growing insecurity, fewer hierarchies, and perpetual and omnipresent danger, these ancient structures of inclusion/exclusion seem to be reinvigorated. But if we look closely, they exhibit the spectral aspect of the moribund who take vengeance on the survivors.

Neither the rampant precariousness of employment nor the contraction of time and space have diminished the need to belong; rather, the experience of belonging more and more resembles the nonplace of birth, where the waters mix and the border between self and other is almost nonexistent, where differences are undetectable and incomprehensible. Where the links, whether with a country, a culture, or a history, seem to evaporate, one finds the individual, aware of his or her singularity but also submerged in the multitude of similar individuals brought into relation, either real or mediated, by globalization.

Some time ago in Milan, an old woman, seated in front of a television screen that opened onto the world, was found dead in her home. Regrettably, she has become the symbol of an epoch characterized by an inability to weave connections and of a society that fails to recognize radically new relations, especially unfamiliar and uncomfortable ones. Her solitary death not only makes visible our belonging to a body that ages and dies, but also reminds us of our close relation with the entire human family.

According to the most astute observers of our time, the paradoxical experience of solitude in the midst of abundant presence characterizes our "temples of consumption"—that is, the shopping mall—a purified "floating space" in which "internal differences are domesticated, sanitized, guaranteed to be free of dangerous ingredients."[3] Places have become non-places; differences are superimposed upon one another as in a kaleidoscope, without impact; the influences of others do not affect our own uniqueness; these meaningless differences now belong to our everyday experience as second nature. One no longer notices the symphony of voices—the senses of humor, the details of personal stories—that suffuses crowded city buses or that echoes from one sidewalk to another. One is no longer where one is; one speaks only to someone standing directly before them; one no longer attends to or values common goods.

Yet, in the "intimacies" of families, couples, and close friends that are now bellowed in public space—a space from which women have been excluded for millennia—anyone willing to listen can hear the passion, joy, and suffering that distinguish and express our humanity rather than our membership in a particular culture.

Today, the "private," albeit in its deformed and deforming representation in advertising and on television, generally delineates new forms of identification and belonging. Intimacy, according to Richard Sennett, may be our last attempt to experience communal moments, even though they may be as fragile as hangers upon which lonely individuals temporarily hang their solitary fears?[4]

In the unending flow of public "confessions," one sees the longing for new links between the individual and the collectivity, between feelings and reason, differentiation and resemblance. Though the locus of our first encounter with another and of all of our subsequent "belonging," the body, and the intimate events that it enables, only now seems to have found a form of citizenship.

We may dislike the way in which television's intimate and visceral content panders to our voyeuristic and exhibitionistic tendencies, but it is not difficult to see that, above the locked rooms of millions of individual spectators, there hovers a question about the essential experiences of life. The success of "reality television" clearly demonstrates our fascination with closed communities and allows us to reflect on the claustrophilic impulse that prompts a group of strangers to share space, for weeks or months, while simultaneously isolating themselves from all personal and historical contexts in order to produce a live-theater experiment featuring cohabitation, love, hate, conflict, and friendship. Despite the evident artificiality of the relations that emerge in such enclosed laboratories, it appears as if psychic life—its basic passions, ancient dramas, its originary cast of characters (i.e., the nucleus of family figures)—can work out its mysteries only in such impersonal and manufactured settings.

The longing for community arises out of a "life made bare"; it can be understood as the desire for solidarity, which can be seen in the willingness of some nations and peoples to take in the masses of stateless persons, refugees, and migrants flooding into all parts of the planet. But this longing can also lead to a narcissistic folding into self in which an individual is willing to violate his or her privacy in order to create new social networks. In a world in which community is no longer determined by proximity or physical reality, the new protagonist is the smartphone. Indispensable for both love and work—long-standing adversaries—the magic box in the palm of one's hand seems ideal for managing seemingly irreconcilable binaries: dependency and freedom, stability and mobility, detachment and perpetual availability.

Perhaps, like Freud's "child with the sprocket," people need to abandon historically burdened relations, risking solitude and indifference, in order to find their way to relations more conscious and free.

The Astuteness of Eros

If Miguel Benasayag and Gérard Schmit's "threat of disaster"[5] now menaces the entire planet, the existential mood of insecurity seems particularly to have infected the West, whose confidence and prosperity are being undermined by poverty and whose universal "values" are increasingly exposed to and challenged by "different" cultures, whose individualism has given way to uncontrolled greed and selfishness, whose technologies are inadequate to meet a changing nature, whose lifestyle has produced "ailments" that flourish behind a mask of perfect health. Describing a state of perpetual instability, sociological analysis invokes images of liquids that "cannot hold a form for any length of time" or of trees that can bend and return to their original positions. Zygmunt Bauman's "liquid modernity,"[6] Richard Sennett's "flexible human being,"[7] and the Precarious Saint of the Disobedient are the new symbols of a society whose foundations are trembling and that knows not whether it will be engulfed by an "apocalyptic night" or be witness to an epochal transformation of the way we live.

At the moment at which time seems to have stopped, when the horizon of the future seems to have disappeared, hope reasserts itself: the irrepressible dream of *utopia* creates new pathways to new possibilities. It is as if, witnessing the end of our own stories and cultures, we are developing the capacity to recognize alternative ways of life. Thus does our "society of risk" simultaneously deploy both fear and hope, weakness and dynamism, nostalgia for community and the empowering of individual autonomy.

The almost daily surveys and statistics that measure the fevered fears of our times raise doubt about whether the promise of a better future can be found in the barbarization of an exhausted society. But the depth and extent of the earthquake that fractured the habits, material certainties, and moral convictions of peoples theretofore certain of their position as the center and measure of the world, as the regulators of chaos, nature, and the human passions, give substance to the hope.

Following the catastrophes of the destruction of the Twin Towers in New York on September 11, 2001, and the tsunami in the South Pacific on December 26, 2004, it was declared that "everything had changed forever," as if a gigantic fault had opened up between reason and an unexplored interiority. But if we shift our view from the world scene to the prosaic and less dramatic "threats" of daily life—the precariousness of work, petty crime, the clash of cultures, climatic disasters, among others—it is not difficult to see that the shaking of long-established certainties can suddenly and radically change one's perspective, can make way for an *other's* inquiring, even disturbing, gaze.

The external sources of contemporary society's widespread anxiety are familiar to most—economic globalization, the constant flow of migrants, climate change and environmental destruction, the crisis of weakening social ties, war and terrorism, the invisible deaths caused by famine, depression, and sickness. It is easier to focus our attention on an external enemy than on internal causes, on our own lives and societies. Like a volcanic eruption, what comes to the surface at a time of crisis is the magma of the uncontrollable effects of history. The alterity that struck at the symbols of global commerce and international tourism—the Twin Towers in New York and the marine paradise of Southeast Asia—was human in the first instance and natural in the second. The socio-politico-economic forces behind both of these sites failed to appreciate the offensiveness of their cultural, social, political, and economic programs of domination and assimilation. The nations and cultures that, until now, have been forced to conform to the western model in order to survive have become, along with the destructive forces of nature, presences that disturb both reason and sleep. We can surrender to the fantasy of an unbearable apocalypse or, instead, we can take responsibility for the imbalances we have created, for the aggression we have inflicted on others; we can move beyond the aggression we have endured and, accepting the fragility and limits of human action, we can orient ourselves toward a new way of being, a new vision of the world.

An analogous shift seems to have occurred in people's personal lives, social relations, and everyday habits. The undermining of certainties that served, for so long, almost as a "second nature," cannot be viewed as arising only from a poverty that is not reducible to the destiny of a social class, from the "feminine" that interrogates historical "differences" between the sexes, from a singularity that frees itself from ancient bonds and subjugation. "Precariousness," "mobility," "risk," "crisis," and "insecurity" detail the consequences of a model of development—capitalist production and consumption—that has become an end in itself and has resulted in a succession of wars, migrations, new forms of slavery, and ecological disasters.

But if economics had not become the primary measure of human life and "flexibility" of work an indicator of social anxiety, it would be obvious to all that to destroy a terrain that appeared to be limited is to destroy the subsoil that one possessed unknowingly, to destroy the *other*, *the different*, who is destined to remain forever silent, who bursts onto the world scene and creates figures, passions, new and unforeseen relations between different cultures and between women and men, individual and collectivity, health and sickness, freedom and dependency, youth and old age, life and death.

Where old borders seemed intractable—borders between private and public, barbarism and civilization, real and artificial, and so forth—new borders emerge. False concepts of nature such as the idea of different destinies for each sex, according to which women were intended to safeguard the continuity of the species and men to "progress" alone in the world, become undone. In a theater dedicated to a vigilant rationality, to power and its institutions and language, the body, with its archaic memory, laws, and wounds, manipulable but also resistant to thought's desire for omnipotence, bursts forth. Men and women, to the extent that they are self-aware, increasingly address matters of the body—they subject it to the practices of modern medicine, they accept its fragility and inevitable end, they anxiously question the promise of science and adopt more natural rhythms, they seek eternal youth, and they demand rights for the "unwanted," including the sick, the elderly, and the disabled. The details of corporeity—different skin color, varying shapes and sizes of the eyes, clothing that signals poverty or cultural difference—also give rise to anxiety. This "interference," which pervades the everyday, from the television screen to the sidewalk and the bus, stirs up issues of "identity" of which one was not previously aware, but to which one now clings as to a defensive weapon.

The emergence of new "worries" goes beyond feelings of anxiety, impotence, fatalism, and beyond the retreat to the utilitarian. The regression that now threatens the advance of progress can be seen, as Elvio Fachinelli put it, as the "historical cunning of eros," which, in order to preserve society, returns to a new barbarism that is believed to guarantee society's further development. As history has already witnessed, "the barbarisms [that arise from human aggression] come from outside a collapsed society in the form of new masses whose subtle operations appear incomprehensible."[8]

Today's bursting forth of alterity stems not only from the worlds that the West colonized and subjected to its own model and to which the West has had to open its doors. It comes as well from the shattering of a long-standing political, economic, sexual, and moral order, which offers an opportunity for the creation of a new equilibrium, new forms of living together, new knowledge and languages. But in order to incorporate difference, to change ideas of what is "real" and "possible," one must not be afraid to analyze the depths of evil while grasping at the same time the contradictory meanings that emerge from the worst disasters.

Though the result of physical forces and laws beyond human control, the tsunami that rocked Southeast Asia undoubtedly raised questions about historically constructed relations: populations whose poverty compels them to offer up their seas for the pleasure of privileged westerners, promises of aid and development from the world's powerful in exchange for the right to exploit human and natural resources, and other unequal exchanges. In addition to the horror of the impossibility of distinguishing the corpses of tourists from those of the locals, among the losses occasioned by the seaquake, we are able to discern the unconscious demarcating line between that part of the world that has the power to assert its values as superior and the rest of the world. Thus do new fears and new awareness arise together, simultaneously producing regression and the discovery of new forms of solidarity. This fear and awareness, this regression and discovery, opens a pathway to perspectives that penetrate to the roots of the human that lie beyond those historical differences that have hindered a perception of ourselves as sharing a common destiny.

Por donde saldrá el sol?

Por donde saldrá el sol? Where will the sun rise? Hope lives in the heart of the night, and as the indigenous peoples of the Americas know, the night can be very long indeed. These peoples define the colonization, attempted genocide, and almost total annihilation of their peoples as a "night" lasting five centuries. Can we, the inheritors of a West that aimed to exterminate them, make their question—*Por donde saldrá el sol?*—our own? "Our epoch is one of crisis.... The new millennium is now fully under way, but misery, sadness, and the suffering of the world have never appeared in such a definitive light."[9]

Miguel Benasayag and Angélique Del Rey conclude their rare book *Elogio del conflitto* [In praise of conflict] by invoking the "multiple dimensions of existence," without which "life can neither be sustained nor can it fully unfold"—an alluring invocation in an age that seems fatally attracted to opposing logics, to simplification and conflict, to identity-based inclusion and exclusion, to the rejection of what is unfamiliar or what lies outside the established order.

What is the "gloom" that seems to be leading the "civilized" West to a new barbarism? Onto what "dangers" does a security-obsessed politics latch itself—a politics in which the measures of "safety" and control, intended to immunize the social body against a widespread and incomprehensible danger, are ever-more invasive? To think in terms of the contradictions and conflicts rooted in the concrete multiplicity of every life is to move beyond the denunciation of a system of power that struggles to defend itself against the wastefulness, garbage, and excesses (both material and human) that it produces. Every protest and act of resistance that wishes not to be merely voluntaristic must address our changing humanity and new interpretative criteria required for wholesale change. As Marco Revelli commented in an interview in *Liberazione*,[10] rather than looking to the past for solutions, "we have to take matters into our own hands."

It is clear that the foreigner, the poor, those "whose appearance or behavior lies outside the norm," the migrant who has been reduced to a state of bare necessity, all incarnate and reveal the originarily "excluded" individuals of a society that, by separating the body from language and biology from history, constructed barriers and blockades even within bodies and psychic life. But these arbitrary divisions are gradually disappearing. The perceived threat, according to Benasayag and Del Rey, also comes from within:

> The core of rationality and wisdom is besieged by uncivilized impulses and passions.... We must learn to live with all that we have excised and abandoned as inadmissible anomalies. We must understand in what way the human being, as s/he is, whose constitutive depths remain obscure, can institute the conditions of communal life *despite* and *through* conflict and thus realize the dream of a better world (or, for those who would prefer to eliminate all that is ungovernable, a nightmare).[11]

Where the logic of utility and efficiency prevails, the entrepreneur and the businessman, according to the norm, seek the meaning of life in "identificatory images of happiness," in the acquisition of cars, vacations, socks, toothpaste, and so on, rather than in the recognition and development of other dimensions of human being. The return of that which has been excluded—the body, the whole and complex life of individuals, the passions, contradictory fantasies—can, of course, be manifested as barbarism, but it can also open up a pathway to desire and productive conflict, to the possibility of redefining social relations in less abstract terms. Simplification and unidimensionality are features of the capitalist system, but they also characterize the politics and programs of the Left as soon as they "depart from the principle according to which all phenomena can be accounted for by the economic reality of the world, an order in which the substrate of all things is understood as a substrate of an economic nature."

Ulrich Beck clearly identifies the awareness that we must bring to political action:

> One's own life is a world that contains in itself all environments.... To be concerned with oneself, to ask oneself pointed questions (Who am I? What do I want? Where am I going?) is an attitude that both the Left and the Right interpret as signaling loss, risk, fallenness, and failure, or, in other words, the original sin of individualism. Other questions arise: In what ways can determined dependencies and interdependencies, which are integral parts of one's own life, interact and

acquire validity in both the political and private spheres? One's own life and, at the same time, global life have become the horizon from which, in the future, we will need to elaborate and justify the concept of life on a social level.[12]

The enormous waste, excess, and garbage that now surround us exceed the significance of the mercantile and consumer systems that produce them. As Guido Viale has observed,[13] "the accumulation of things that we do not need and the discarding of all that no longer interests or attracts us" represent a privileged way of being and thinking, a way that sets no limit on indulgence and fears loss. But we must look at what trails behind history in the darkness: the potential and capacities of human beings have been deformed and rendered unrecognizable by their long exclusion. But if we uncover and refocus our attention on this potential, individual and collective experiences can emerge in their complexity as contradictory, multiplex, and conflictual, and we can begin to rethink power, both in its visible, macroscopic forms and as it is manifested in the ways individuals and communities think and live. This can lead us to a different way of perceiving and establishing value than that now found in institutional and social relations, in political organizations and movements.

> The centralizing roles of the institutions of macropower have contributed to the entrenchment of the idea that institutions constitute the place from which the life of a society is directed, but, in reality, the situation is otherwise. Paradoxically, the mechanism of centralization ascribes a peripheral function to institutions. Macropower does not encompass political and social processes. Centralization is an archive or a secondary expression/form. It is not political power, nor is politics enclosed, oriented, or directed by the supposed power of centralization. Rather, it is at the level of multiplex processes of power and through the negotiation of conflict within the structures of micropower that the most radical changes to ways of life and to the mechanisms of social reproduction are realized.[14]

Practices that subvert power, therefore, can be used not only by associations, NGOs, and committees but can be deployed in the domains of art, medicine, education, urban planning, sport—indeed, in all complex processes. Such practices serve to prevent any particular political group or avant-garde movement exhibiting a directive tendency from being taken up by a political party. This kind of approach, as Benasayag and Del Rey observe, "is not generally accepted by traditional militants, who see in it the risk of dispersion." This kind of "circumscribed action" also permits one to see current conflicts while recognizing the illusory nature of any given situation.

We are structured to act and think in any situation, and as we must always and necessarily act without complete knowledge and information, we cannot, therefore, foresee all the consequences of and reactions to our own actions. The strong model of practical politics proposed here is able simultaneously to renounce universal solutions and to provide a unifying perspective by taking into account the multiplicity of our actions. The acceptance of conflict, unlike the prevailing logic of war, which thrives on fear, revenge, and persecution of the enemy, is, therefore, the acceptance of life in all of its manifestations. The temptation to ascribe to a "subject" a reticular movement attributable to an alternative way of being appears when the analyses of the "decisive," driving force of the struggles of the "have-nots"—those without permanent homes or work, those violently excluded—stop. People in such situations desire only what they lack and what others possess. Different from the proletariat, women, ethnic and sexual minorities, these figures of social dis-ease lack the "promise" that grants respect to other marginalized groups in terms of belonging and participation, both explicit and implicit, in the whole of society. It is essential, then, that we "construct a common base between the various have-nots, a category of a different kind, whose definition must not be limited to the lack of certain goods."[15]

This condition of exclusion, which affects the most diverse members of society—from the migrant to the researcher who defends her science against the demand for utility, from the artist to the teacher to the unemployed—is spreading. In this expansion, the have-nots, who "embody the point at which the promise of modernity is turned upside down," are located at the heart of our times. By virtue of their very existence, the dispossessed expose the defect of the system, namely, the impossibility of the universal extension of modernity's "promise" to all.

As Benasayag has noted elsewhere, the "materiality of the new century," to borrow Marco Revelli's expression, offers an original and effective perspective that can bring to light the multiple and contradictory faces of a new kind of power that can weave together production and various modes of life, social relations and personal experiences, sexuality and politics. Consequently, many different forms of rebellion, dissension, conflict, and resistance can be manifested in society's external borders and its internal rules and regulations as well as in the norms of society that act invisibly upon our lives as embodied imperatives.

Against this horizon, which shifts the borders of politics and pushes them to the roots of the human, a new perspective emerges—a perspective that encourages and incorporates a variety of movements in which unexpected connections and creative capacities allow us to intuit a new way of being and living, as they did in '68 when the body, the individual, and social relations became indistinguishable from the revolutionary process itself.

Chapter Five

The Unstoppable Revolution

A Room of Thoughts

After more than forty years of living in Milan, the city remains for me the place one comes to from elsewhere. Returning to the city now, one feels compelled to avert one's eyes in shame from the visible degradation, and then, suddenly and unexpectedly, one feels embraced by an inviting and vibrant space. Born a woman in a countryside drenched in misery following the Second World War and given the gift of education at the local secondary school (*liceo*), I had the painful privilege of building intellectual walls to protect myself from the untutored voices of my parents. In Milan, the "room" of ideas that had welcomed an adolescent fleeing uncomfortable country roots expanded to embrace a graying city that was both too full and too empty, much like the interior of a factory.

Arriving in Milan at my earliest opportunity, I was ready to relinquish the construct of myself as daughter, student, wife, and teacher of an unspoken "morality"—constructed over a period of twenty-five years—and be reborn. As the place of my rebirth, Milan, with its train station, its streets, and its benches, became my dormitory: it seemed like a maternal body, dilated and anonymous; it was mysterious and filled with a terrible darkness that prevented one from sleeping; though never really far from one's home, one often confused the seemingly familiar outline of a hedge or a line of poplars with death. The sudden abandonment of the habitual and conventional, like a natural catastrophe, transforms familiar people and things into unrecognizable detritus that renders memory indifferent.

No return is possible for those who sever unquestioned relations. And if some trace of "home" remains in one's thoughts, it is dismissed as a joke or as a source of entertainment. Though it may at first appear as consoling and attractive, home is not a haven. Memories of my early years in Milan fray into fine details—street corners, the interiors of bars, telephone booths—like the tiles of a shifting mosaic that constitutes a vivid emotional landscape. And within a few years of my moving to my new city and living a newly dramatic and exhilarating life, I joined world-shaking movements such as those of 1968, which challenged borders of all sorts. Belonging to this or that place seemed to have forever lost its heavy legacy of fatality.

I am not sure I know how to say what Milan meant to me in the decade that saw women move en masse into public squares and neighborhoods, convinced that the time of family, public authority, and private suffering had come to an end. I remember the speeches, the thoughts scribbled on flyers or in the margins of newspapers, now preserved in the archives; I remember the names of streets—Via Cherubini, Via Col di Lana—and the places that hosted meetings, acquaintances, loves. Feminism, with its itinerant groups that moved between homes and broad collective settings, further transformed the map of an expanding territory that had taken on the face of our own projects and our expectations of change.

A decade later and a few square meters larger, my house, packed almost to the rafters with paper, served as the home for two journals: first, *L'erba voglio*, which was followed by *Lapis: Percorsi della riflessione femminile*. As a single woman, I gave many speeches; my life was very public and filled with people. To my parents, I remained an eternal student.

For me, "a room of one's own" was found on noisy streets illuminated by the light of Milan's rare blue skies; there, I became accustomed to living inside myself as well as in the world. At first, I conjured other landscapes in my mind's eye. Later, through friendships and collaborative projects in other cities and countries, I came to love these landscapes. Borders, which both separate and join, are precious precisely because they offer a solitude that fosters a capacity for intense society and renders one's window an observatory from which to contemplate reality and its constituent, distant aspects.

Milan is all of these things—so much more than a city of polluted and foul-smelling air, of proliferating tumors, of poisoned souls.

Dissident Desire

"The revolution, like desire, is inevitable and cannot be avoided: it will never cease to shake up the guardians of the domain of needs." Thus did Elvio Fachinelli describe the "brief, intense, and exclusive" summer of 1968.[1]

What are the needs to which politics today must respond? Are they the "objective," "structural" needs of economic globalization and a moribund model of development? Or are they "subjective" needs—needs that seem to surprise the Left because they fall outside the idea of "materiality," which has been mutilated by essentialized aspects of the human? And where is desire? Has it been devoured by a consumerist spasm, by the pervasiveness of the media, by the defense of private wealth? Does desire continue to work underground? Ignored by both the Left and the Right, our desires remain unheard and unseen. Is the resurgence of that most ancient reflex—the fear of difference, of the stranger—merely the repetition of a familiar phenomenon, or is it the manifestation of a "barbarism" that distorts the inescapable and radical demands of the present in a dangerous way? The defeats suffered by the Left in recent years have inevitably produced a return to well-known but lost "territories," which inevitably mark a return to old and often empty ideas, strategies, and relationships.

In *Liberazione*, Flore Murard-Yovanovitch argued that

> the Left as a system of ideas has been defeated, in part, because it did not think beyond the ideas of the "society of work and the economized society...." This period is almost historic in that it offers new and alternative social experiences. Society trembles with a million proposals, if one cares to listen: we need (instead of the language of needs) new social relations and a new way of living.

Thousands of inventive practices and methods are being created by ordinary citizens: networks for the recycling of objects, exchanges of expertise, social ecology networks, community centers, groups of people choosing to live with very little. These movements manifest "a politics of refusal of the economization of life" in everyday life. They place human relations and free time at the center of life.[2]

When one observes the split between social identity and political subjectivity—for example, in the case of workers who vote for the Right—one implicitly recognizes that the individual and the citizen are not aligned. Indeed, Tocqueville remarked that the citizen is the individual's worst enemy. But this split also signifies that the individual no longer identifies with his or her professional status, territory, or sexually assigned role within a couple or a family. The essence of politics, which has always been the primary motor of social conflict and transformation, has now been reduced to a politics of the individual—an individual increasingly disconnected from its embeddedness in social relations.

To claim that the lived experience of a single individual consists of a constellation of confused needs, identities, places, relations, passions, fantasies, and competing interests and desires is to recognize that there is a "territory" that lies beyond the borders of public life. Lived experience, which includes psychic life—a realm of borders between the domains of the unconscious, between body and thought, a realm whose depths remain largely unexplored—is not reducible to the social. The racist, xenophobic, and misogynist "viscera" to which the antipolitics of the Right appeals is the sediment of barbarism, ignorance, and ancient prejudice, and of dreams and desires that have been ignored, especially by the Left, which remains stubbornly anchored in the primacy of work and the working class. It is imperative to remember that, following the great shift in consciousness introduced by Marx, other radical challenges and insights were presented by psychoanalysis, feminism, the nonviolence movement, biopolitics, and environmentalism.

Subjectivity and the person, understood as the experience of a single individual as a thinking body, outside of the obligatory relations of family and community, have made headway only with great effort. They have now assumed a form of individualism that precludes solidarity, and, as a result, left-wing parties and movements have become divided and look upon one another with suspicion. For those who, in the 1970s, were focused on safeguarding the great "unity of the classes," "the personal is political" sounded like a "bourgeois" slogan. Today, those who champion the metropolitan dimension of the political, who fight for the rights of their fellow human beings—for gays and lesbians, women, and migrants—are designated *radical chic*.

But it is also the direct testimony of individuals, the reason and sense offered by voices outside traditional public debate and the political class, that give form to the often-invoked "social." We cannot ignore this reason and sense if we truly wish to construct a less violent and less alienated society.

Tiziana Gentilizi, a young worker at Zanussi at Forlì,[3] described her work in an interview published by the journal *Una Città*:

> The important thing is not to speak about your work, which is slightly depressing.... One speaks of one's vacations, of what one bought, of "Big Brother." In the workplace, one is isolated.... The young people who come to the factory probably do so out of necessity. Everyone has their own story. But everyone, or, at least, the great majority, see working in the factory as temporary, so they are not much interested in the fact of being workers.... There is no longer a deep sharing of work. The important thing is to complete one's eight hours in the most tranquil way possible, and who gives a shit about tomorrow anyway? We will see. On the positive side, working there allows one to think about other things; one can even listen to music on a Walkman. Today, the worker feels less like a worker. Individual strategies prevail.[4]

As Ernst Bloch once said, "One cannot live by bread alone, especially if one does not have any." Were the workers on the assembly lines of a big Milanese factory such as Alfa Romeo of Arnese in the 1970s so different from today's workers? Did they not discuss politics? According to one worker of that era,

> Assembly-line work imposes a rhythm on you; even when you have finished your work day, you cannot stop moving. You cannot concentrate on anything serious, so you do stupid, silly things with your coworkers instead—shove that guy, hit another, and yell at a third, and so forth. You do all of this to feel alive.... Exhausted by work, you and your work friends seek to escape reality, and the comic book becomes the master of your fantasies.... At times, one dreams with one's eyes wide open....
>
> ... To truly be able to work with people, to concretely be able to touch people, one needs, and I am not being ironic here, to pass through one's own dreams.[5]

The "short" season of '68, and the movements that followed in the next decade—especially the nonauthoritarian movement that gave birth to feminism and the journal *L'erba voglio*—saw the arrival of *unexpected subjects* in the public scene. Women and other young people brought with them new analyses and the political practices of the Marxist tradition and workers' movements. These new subjects not only came into conflict with the established parties of the Left, but also contested the idea of revolution itself. Elvio Fachinelli offered the most astute reading of this rupture with the Left. In "Il desiderio dissidente," published in 1968 in the journal *Quaderni piacentini*, he brought to light the student movement's early focus on liberation and antiauthoritarianism. In "Gruppo chiuso o gruppo aperto?," published later that same year, he predicted the sectarianism that would subsequently afflict these movements and the birth of multiple parties and groups with a Marxist-Leninist orientation. In one of his most important essays, "Il paradosso della ripetizione" [The paradox of repetition], he explained why the same mechanisms of domination and submission, the same passivity and the desire for a leader that characterized the "old politics" would be reproduced in the new:

> The difficulty of Marxism vis-à-vis '68 arose from the fact that these new "masses" were demanding revolution but hadn't yet entered the

system of social production; they were not, therefore, immediately and clearly framed in terms of class.... I called their different logic of behavior in relation to the real and the possible "dissenting desire."... The initial, and I would say, genetic, aspect of the movement opposed the logic of the satisfaction of needs that was dominant at the time.[6]

Fachinelli understood very well that *need* and *desire* are always present, one in the other, but that it is necessary to distinguish them in order to avoid the devolution of the new form of revolution, expressed in the dissidence of the youth movement, into old schemata. The desire unleashed by the youth movement, less materialistic than the politics of the time, was also politically shrewder.

The idea of revolution held by many Marxists consists in the following: an upheaval of the masses produced by their needs, an upheaval that would be consciously analyzed by the party as it seized power.... But this notion failed to consider anything beyond these narrowly defined "needs" of the masses and the hegemonic reason of the party. The extraordinary crushing of the masses, theoretically and practically brought about by the imposition of a limited and totalizing ideology, became clear at the appearance of a hint of revolution. The student movement was such a hint; it was motivated by a logic *different* than that of previous revolutionary movements.[7]

The initial phases of the movement, then, were characterized by what Fachinelli called "a process of communalization" on the part of a "desiring group," which succeeded in overcoming the ancient reflex that regarded the stranger as an enemy. By attempting to crush dissidents, the powers-that-be affirm and strengthen their bonds, unifying them in a community of like-minded others. Soon, however, the unifying thrust of the movement began to fray in the face of the difficulties created by its growth and success; internal disputes, "clarification," and purification led to groups closing in on themselves.

The emergence of "unexpected" subjects in the public domain, women in particular, was a symptom of the "crisis of politics" at the time and heralded the beginning of a rethinking of politics. This crisis was, of course, inscribed in the very founding of the polis, but it was thrown into relief at the moment the relations between public and private, home and polis, were being challenged. That which had been "banned" suddenly appeared on the public agenda. As Rossana Rossanda put it, the "deep waters of the person" as well as the "secret material" of nature and history returned from their long exile. Despite the denial of female subjectivity, the "extreme protest of feminism" engendered a conflict in the revolutionary movement. What, Rossanda mused, "would happen to institutions when they were forced to realize that they served only one sex?"[8]

To recognize that consumer society had changed the boundaries between the personal and public spheres was to recognize that dualistic interpretative schema as well as the forms of knowledge derived from them had rendered both the individual and society, as well as the elements of other dualisms, abstract and ideological. It was necessary to abandon dualism itself in order to seek the connections between formerly exclusive terms, and this is what Fachinelli did in his articles of 1968. For doing so, he was scolded by both Marxists, for whom the truth of the individual can only be found in the togetherness of social and objective relations, and by psychoanalysis, "which focused on certain essential aspects of the individual, but found itself disarmed by increasingly totalitarian methods aimed at the formation of individuals and groups."[9]

Private life was increasingly permeated by public life, and this resulted in the politicization of personal relationships. "Massification" meant the social atomization of individuals and "functionalism," that is, their subjection to a "system whose regulation they already anticipated." This decreasing distance between private and public life has, in recent years, been reflected in the increasing recurrence of the word "integration." According to Fachinelli, behind the contestation of the authoritarian father, a figure that has largely faded away, lies a more remote target, the fantasy of a society that combines the prospect of security with the "loss of self as subject and desire." At the height of its development, consumer society seems to configure itself imaginatively as both the satisfying and the devouring mother, who offers food in exchange for an absolute dependency that induces a sense of impotence and anguish.

The nonauthoritarian teachers' movement emerged just before the student movement, and after the Milan conference Umanitaria in June and September of 1970, the nonauthoritarian movement itself became an important national reference for the students. *L'erba voglio*[10] came out of this conference, as did an anonymous journal (1971–1978). An important antecedent to these events was a radical course devoted to alternative forms of pedagogy at the State University of Milan in the winter of 1968–1969, in which Elvio Fachinelli was a key participant. It was in this course that the idea of a self-directed child day care arose, and the day care opened in January 1970 at Porta Ticinese in Milan. In the student document that addressed the necessity of a "model institution for collective education," one can still detect the air of '68, especially in its polemic with the "false revolutionaries," who were quick to distance themselves by creating their own groups. As the students described them, these "false revolutionaries" were afraid of living, incapable of freedom, and craved protection; they longed for "leaders and myths."

The declared objective was the recovery of a politics "related to the body, connected to the biological dimension of individuals," always keeping in mind that the inculcation of "authoritarianism, which begins in the family during infancy, produces well-adjusted but discouraged characters."[11] Even when adults do not intervene in children's interactions in an authoritarian way, "an unyielding hierarchy based on strength and power, which stamps itself on children's relations with one another," is clearly evident. As Fachinelli, in "Masse a tre anni" [The masses at three years of age], commented, "One seems to find oneself in a violent society, somewhere between the fascist and the mafioso, [observing] a relation in which the strongest and most powerful protect one's own." He concluded that "the only liberatory politics is a radical politics, understood in the Marxian sense of 'grabbing mankind by the roots.' "[12]

L'erba voglio, a selection of the material published in the journal, was published as a book in 1971 and featured writings by teachers, students, workers, and psychologists on the personal difficulties and perplexities that arise from nonauthoritarian practices. The book's intent was not to devise new pedagogies or teaching strategies, but "to stabilize liberating relations without concern for preconstituted functions and competencies, to allow education to move beyond the restrictive gates and walls of its institutions, to remove education from its masters, to 'make school' with *others*." The book's preface highlighted the increasing bureaucratization of the relations of power and the increasing subjection of individuals to the "anonymous coercion of power." It remarked the extent of "depersonalization" and the beginning of "mass slavery." It argued that, in order to constitute a different society, it was necessary to attend to the individual from infancy, to the family, to day care, because the attitudes and values that produced passivity and the delegation of responsibility, and those that could produce cooperation and consensus-building, were established in these settings. Authoritarianism needed to be held accountable for its treatment of those most defenseless, namely, for the education of the child.

School, seen as a separate place for the transmission of knowledge and unrelated to production, was restored to the masses by the reconsideration, reformulation, and, in some instances, the rejection of those practices that necessarily excluded them: the top-down mode of relaying information, exclusionary language, bureaucratization, the rigid definition of competencies, nepotism, the obligation to endure in silence. The greatest goal was to construct "relations of equality" such that no one would hold power over another, to foster independence and anticipate or invent a different society through collective labor. It was believed that utopia could be achieved.

If utopia was to be achieved, it was necessary to remove the conditions that create passivity, to relinquish the division between those who command and those who obey. The practice of the assembly in which all were empowered to speak was intended to guarantee "equality among those who are different," "egalitarian participation in the determination of content, roles, and the scheduling of school activities."

Above all, the need to *become conscious* of the coercion and domination that, though exclusively attributed to others, rapidly reappear in one's own behavior because of early inscription and interiorization, became essential. Taking into account the importance of one's absolute dependency on others during the first years of life led us to reflect on the magnitude of negative experience that had accumulated in the history of this century in which the foundation of change had been exclusively understood as a function of the relations of production.

Nonauthoritarian practice was both "distributive and liberatory": it rejected the rules to which traditional educational practices conformed (that is, grades, passing and failing, etc.), and affirmed the development of the creative capacities of all. With respect to education, "the achievable utopia" consisted of the investment of the "conception and exercise of power, of the power to decide and to execute, in all; the separation of the minority that controlled society for its own ends from the excluded masses was to be overcome, not in a renewed view of school as a happy island, but through a political process that resolved to hold as its essential commitment the end of passivity and fear, the presence and participation of all those theretofore excluded by power, the regular practice of public assembly, collective decision-making, the exercise of power shared among equal and autonomous individuals."[13] Not surprisingly, many of the texts in *L'erba voglio* (book) established the grounds for the extension of nonauthoritarian practices to other forms of oppression.

Rereading Rudi Dutschke's interview of May 1968 in *Quaderni piacentini*, one is struck by the similarity between his views and those expressed in *L'erba voglio*. According to Dutschke, the communist parties feared integration. Social transformation would be possible only if the masses were to take their own destinies in hand; Dutschke urged them to create their own autonomous organizations in different institutions (factories, universities, schools, churches), even if those institutions were themselves authoritarian and characterized by authoritarian structures and personalities. The anti-authoritarian struggles that were being fought in the universities would produce intellectual changes and changes in character, new attitudes toward life and society. Dutschke was speaking of real and direct democracy, which opposes the society that "administers individuals in an increasingly totalizing way." The movement would, he thought, extend itself "in the long march through [other] institutions," to society itself. At the end of the interview, Dutschke declared that the struggle could not be understood simply as an "economic struggle," noting that "[the struggle] was being led by factions that did not occupy a determined place in material production—that is, university students and secondary schools."

Similarly, the journal *L'erba voglio*, which began publishing when the revolutionary movements of 1968 had already begun to fragment into closed and sectarian factions with hierarchical structures like those of the traditional parties, advocated the "logic of desire" and the "communalization" that had emerged in '68, which sought to incorporate diverse social groups such as students, teachers, workers, and artists. For those of us who were helping to form feminist groups at the time, 1968 marked the beginning of a fecund period that lasted for a decade—a period that we must not allow to be overshadowed by the terrorism that followed.

The editorial notes in the first volumes of *L'erba voglio* defined the spirit of the journal as a whole:

> We do not presume to act as a central committee aligned with a specific party. We believe that we are capable of carrying on serious political work.... Unfortunately, this approach was adopted by many in the avant-garde who nonetheless found themselves once again marginalized in the ghetto ... of an unhappy Left frozen in its own impotence and beaten down by an always-distant revolution.[14]

Ever mindful of distant readers who responded to the journal by means of its enclosed reply card, the journal sought to establish an open and flexible connection with others and to speak more than one language:

> We began from the recognition that there are forces available in different cities across many regions. Core regional groups could become centers of discussion and places in which to share common experiences. Obviously, the relation between these core groups and the group in Milan was one of equality. It seems, however, that in this

first phase, the Milan group constituted a point of reference.... It was therefore incumbent upon us to transmit and retransmit information and ideas, and to respond to requests, and so forth.

The aim, then, was to hold "different voices in a common togetherness," without a rigid ideological framework but according to certain general rules: personal responsibility, remaining faithful "to one's own intimate experience," using one's own condition as one's starting point, and rethinking social ties on the basis of a new materiality (an embodied subjectivity). The journal proposed new forms of action and interaction, new ways of negotiating conflict and criticism, new ways of communicating and a new language, all in the hope of restoring pleasure to our daily lives. We dreamed of a form of action that itself could manifest the capacity for change and resolve the separation between the (impossible) dream and (a more than possible) reality, thus eliminating the need for the dream itself. If politics isolated one in an aristocratic "fort" and forced one to resort to a rigid moralism, it was because politics ignored "everyday communal experience." Distinguishing between what was and was not political—the latter being discounted as insignificant—both increased women's sense of impotence and estrangement from society and simultaneously transformed the dream into a program for action that could produce meaningful change.

As Luisa Muraro remarked, the "zone of darkness" that women inhabited, whether according to the official story or revolutionary theory, was not an indication of their limitations; rather, it indicated the inadequacy of politics vis-à-vis the complexity of experience.

> The life of a human being is more than his/her place in production. We know this on account of concrete experience, inscribed in us by the hours we spend at play, making love, remembering, forgetting.... The separation between man and woman, the domination of the latter by the former, has amputated humanity from the human being.... This true and genuine dehumanization..., though different than that produced by the exploited labor of the individual, is not inferior to it.[15]

Criticizing the military, which always targets an "other," such as the worker or the developing world, for example, one reader asked: "Is the subject a self, a person?" Taking oneself as the starting point, which necessarily includes the body and sexuality, firmly situated the journal in the women's movement. And despite the eventual fragmentation that splintered feminism into multiple factions and fractured the editorial group to which Luisa Muraro and I belonged, this grounding in the embodied self caused a radical crisis for traditional politics.

Some of the first groups of feminists in Italy took shape in universities that had been occupied by the students. They thus found themselves inside a revolutionary movement, that, at least initially, was nonauthoritarian—a movement that, although it was intended to fight exploitation, alienation, assimilation into the system, and other forms of domination, failed to consider the first and most ancient form of all domination, namely, that of the feminine by the masculine. It also failed to consider the deep alienation from one's own being implicit in the exclusive identification of woman with the body, nature, and sexual and reproductive functions. The radical question about the double exploitation of women had already been documented by Demau, a Milanese group that began to meet in 1967.

> The attribution of different and determined roles to women and men is completely essentializing, whether it comes from the material functions of the mechanism of capitalism (private property) or from its system of determining value. This system of determining value exalts the spirit of entrepreneurship, which is no more than a taste for and a cult of violence, no more than male "supremacy," which finds in the conception of the "female" both the concept's legitimacy and its very foundation.[16]

To the extent that culture and the system of production were founded on precise relations of production that were rooted in a specific notion of male and female social roles, women were inserted into a system and a culture that were developed without them. Feminism was thus required to radically redefine the political. But in the struggle for women's emancipation as well as in the revolutionary Left, it quickly became clear that women needed to distance themselves from men. Even in those liberatory struggles and groups, the relation between the sexes remained unchanged, often unchallenged, and women continued to occupy traditional roles. The need for *separatism* was evident. Feminism restored to the polis not only the *body*, but the *sexed* body, on which the different destinies of men and women were based. Separatism was, above all, a search for models of *autonomy* that could be internalized, for an alternative to a vision of the world that had been produced by men. It enabled the construction of a sociality between women that was not mediated by the masculine gaze, which restricted women to being "mothers of," "wives of," and "daughters of."

Mainstream society framed the analysis of male domination as a "woman's question"—that is, a matter of disadvantages and discrimination—that belonged to the personal sphere: the body, sexuality, and maternity, all of which constituted the primary and originary locus of the expropriation of female being—the annihilation of female sexuality, female individuality, and political existence. The restriction of women to a biological role was taken to be the foundation of women's submission and dedication to men and their willingness to sacrifice their selfhood.

Somewhat differently, we spoke of "liberation" rather than "liberty," of an originary "differentiation," which underlies all dualisms, rather than "difference." We sought the roots of male violence, of the social marginalization of women, and of the exploitation of domestic work in the lived, sexed, loved body, in sickness, and in madness. We analyzed, above all, *invisible violence*, which we understood as the presupposition for all other forms of violence and oppression. "Reappropriation of the body" meant recognizing and legitimating one's own sexuality while, at the same time, reconfiguring the idea of health outside of and apart from the invasive practices of medical science.

"Speaking for oneself," which signified one's entry into the polis, entailed a tenacious adherence to the body and the internal world, which led one to rediscover the enduring traces of history, themselves inherently political. Next, we began to examine historical constructions of male society, including the family, forms of knowledge and power, the institutions of public life, as well as those territories, such as personal history and unconscious formations, which were regarded as apolitical and rediscovered by feminist practice.

This practice, and the discoveries to which it led, necessitated our abandonment of dualism; seeking *connections* between sexuality and politics, sexuality and the symbolic, we came to recognize that sexuality belonged to both the private and public spheres. Likewise, in economic terms, we unmasked the free labor performed by women, which passed under the guise of love and care. We exposed the gaps between so-called objective reality and personal, lived experience.

Rossana Rossanda, however, intuited that these "deep waters" could once again serve to exclude us from public life or lead to nothing more than a few democratic concessions. Feminism in the 1970s is almost always misremembered as the struggle to acquire certain rights vis-à-vis divorce, family relations and property, abortion, women's health clinics. One easily recalls the protests, which many extra-parliamentary groups characterized as a "coming out." Regarded as anomalous in terms of traditional politics and dismissed as a kind of "feminist vacation," self-consciousness and conscious-raising were integral to feminist practice, in which the body, sexuality, homosexuality, and the development of collective thinking were central. Women's health and medicine as well as abortion were also central. None of us wanted abortion or divorce to be "reduced to a piece of reform, to be considered in isolation from the dominant sexuality and social structure that had rendered woman a machine for reproduction."

The feminist movement sought modes of relation that were very similar to those advocated in the journal *L'erba voglio*: the structures of both were antiauthoritarian and liberatory, and "becoming aware" and "speaking for oneself" were important. As the body, lived experience, and the story of each individual were paramount, it became evident that traditional organizational forms would not suffice.

With *Sottosopra*, for some years Italy's preeminent feminist journal, the Via Cherubini collective of Milan offered women a point of reference, a means of sharing women's experiences; it wanted to offer a "living alternative" to the traditional role of woman. Unlike standard newspapers or other instruments of propaganda, the collection and sharing of women's experiences helped to motivate individual responsibility and personal activity. Foregoing editorial selection and accepting all submissions, and not wishing "to become an instrument for the good management of the written word, [the members of the collective] served as editors for one another."[17]

It is not possible to underestimate the power of the word in political groups, to which many feminists belonged; the word, in most political organizations, was, for women, "the instrument of exclusion." Moreover, it was difficult to take the measure of oneself with a language that had been elaborated by men and that reflected matters as they appeared to men. But feminist practice transformed the word into an "instrument of affirmation."

Despite their different contexts, there was overlap between the theory and practice of nonauthoritarian movements and feminism. Feminism spoke of shifting the border between the personal and public spheres, of the tendency of consumer society to infiltrate every aspect of life, of its depersonalizing effects, of the voracity of a system that erases the individual as desire and that leads to the "passivity of the masses."

Even though they were often misidentified as "ethically sensitive questions," matters usually regarded as "nonpolitical," to which these movements brought attention—the body, sexuality, maternity, health, birth, family relationships, and so on—were repositioned at the heart of politics.

After a centuries-old exile, the body now took its revenge: personal life invaded the public scene; it both absorbed and was absorbed by public life. Today, the body is subject to opposing forces: on one hand, *biopower* persecutes the biological body (above all, the female body), and this biopower is supported by the powers of the state and the church, as well as by science, the biotechnology industry, and the media. On the other hand, the body now dominates the public sphere, which seems to have been devoured by all that it believed it had "banned": politics has been absorbed by television as entertainment, work has become "feminized," and the polis is confused with the home and the firm.

Patriarchal power, obscured by its institutional clothing, has been reinvigorated in a familiar form: a figure, both threatening and protective, that represses and subjugates. "Governability" replaces political democracy, rendering conflict ineffective. The state's insistence on security, the rise of racism, xenophobia, homophobia, and misogyny expose the ancient, unconscious, collective reflex: the "other" is the enemy, a scapegoat. The first "other," of course, who appears at birth, is the female body, and this differentiation tells us much about the "sovereign power" that divides and opposes the masculine and the feminine, the body and thought, biology and history, the individual and society.

From the perspective of remaking *sense*, of fostering participation in politics, which has become increasingly self-referential and divorced from daily life, the *lessons of '68* and the movements that characterized that era are instructive. They constituted the most radical attempt to initiate a discussion about reforming society from its very foundations—that is, a discussion about *sexism*, the founding act of politics, which excluded the entire female sex from all decision-making power. By foregrounding the body, the experience and implications of infancy, personal life, and the relation between the sexes, and releasing them from their long confinement in the prison of the "unpolitical," a novel and unprecedented point of view became available, a point of view that, rereading the history of humanity, understood male domination as the original structure of all forms of power. This point of view catalyzed institutional upheaval far more radical than that anticipated by Rudi Dutschke in 1968.

The apparent aphasia of the Marxist *operaismo* stemmed from the Left's inability to renew its interpretative paradigms. It lacked a politics rooted in the "whole of life," including the sexual division of labor; male-female relations; the adult-child relation; the family as the locus of the institutionalization of a dependency, begun in infancy, that naturalizes the sexual and reproductive role of women and thereby fixes the relations between nature and culture, and between individual and society, as oppositional and complementary. In order to confront the atomization of the masses, it is necessary to interrogate lives as they are lived, the actual experiences of individuals, their relations with the structures of power, with forms of knowing, and with the institutions of public life—what is now referred to as the "viscera" [innards] of history, ignored and neglected by the Left, and regarded with contempt and cynicism by the Right.

One forgets, or perhaps wishes not to recognize, that the nonauthoritarian and feminist movements marked the beginning of an "affirmative biopolitics," a politics that accorded a greater role to the body, a politics that questioned experience and understood subjectivity as located in the thinking, sexed, and plural body rather than as belonging to the abstract figure of the citizen. This thinking-body subject would simultaneously be able to recognize its singularity and its community with others; it would be able to access a more general horizon while, at the same time, penetrating the deep layers of the individual's memory.

The Salvific Bilingualism of the Political Culture of Women

It is incomprehensible that the political culture produced by women's insightful reflections over a period of forty years has remained largely invisible and marginal, especially in view of the fact that the many themes foregrounded by the women's movement now occupy center stage in public life.

The roots of the current crisis of politics continue to lie in the founding act of politics and its consequences—the sexual division of labor, the separation of body and language, individual and society. The preeminence of the body, sexuality, health, birth and death, male violence against women, the relation with the other—contemporary public life affects all of these essential human experiences. If it is true that feminism—the peaceful revolution—was the only survivor of the revolutionary 1970s, the only revolution that continued to unfold, proliferating into a vast array of groups, associations, cultural and political centers, it is also true that it quietly oscillated between brief appearances and quick disappearances.

The political action and thought of the women's movement have deepened and become more radical in response to the needs of our historical context. An antidote to populism, to the triumph of antipolitics, and to the reawakening of religious fundamentalism, it may be that feminist practice and forms of knowing can offer us a genuine *politics of life*.

The question, then, is why feminist culture failed to become universal. Clearly, it involves and pertains to both men and women, to both public and private spheres. So why, despite our knowledge and insight—insight indispensable for understanding our current upheavals—do we now feel ourselves to be "poor"?

Women, identified with the body, nature, sexual and reproductive functions, and thus excluded from the responsibilities of public life, indeed, from the very status of "human," continue to be considered the "object" of knowledge. In addition to the particular powers of the historical community of men, it has been male forms of knowledge that have defined the "female" and have, more or less directly, controlled, exploited, enacted violence upon, and contrarily, imaginarily exalted, the bodies as well as the psychic and intellectual lives of women. Violence is not only physical. Revealing the lines of domination, violence is also manifest in forms of knowledge, most insidiously (because invisible) in the interiorization of a self-image dictated by others: a way of thinking about oneself, a way of feeling and being derived from another's language and vision of the world. When Rousseau, the father of modern democracy, excluded women from the "social contract," when he described female purpose and destiny as service, as the pleasing of and being useful to men, he was able to take for granted the common feeling of women, a feeling forged through adaptation and the need to survive. In order to do so, women learned to make themselves indispensable to men, and to employ their power of attraction through seduction and maternity.

Breaking free of this burdensome historical legacy has produced two effects: the false neutrality of male ways of knowing has been unmasked, and what Sibilla Aleramo at the turn of the twentieth century called "the representation of an a priori world" has been revealed and analyzed. What Aleramo accomplished in solitude—the analysis of male domination through a process of "unveiling" and the elaboration of the "autonomy of female being"—became, in the feminism of the 1970s, the practice of consciousness-raising, which consisted of a deep probing of the self, the modification of a deep psychic balance ("becoming conscious"), and the construction of the self as a complete individual—a thinking body whose thought was embodied and sexed.

The 1970s, then, saw not only the massive entry of women into public life (work outside the home, education, urbanization, political engagement, etc.) and the birth of a *female, singular, and plural subjectivity*; it witnessed a peaceful revolution that illuminated what had been naturalized as human and had become fossilized. This revolution subverted traditional ideas of politics and questioned the historical construction of society by men, beginning with the assumptions that underpin society—assumptions rooted in the biological and based upon an *originary scission* from which the subsequent dualisms with which we are all too familiar were constructed; the primary division from which all other divisions flow is the bifurcation of male and female.

Through a new consciousness and a female voice, a different conception of culture, history, democracy, freedom, and politics came to the fore. This conception was not merely another "form of knowledge" that could be added to other, preexisting forms; it was not an injection of knowledge that could be incorporated into existing knowledge or be used to "fertilize the sterile society of men." This was not a matter of complementarity—it was, rather, a radical departure from the ideas that had accompanied the struggle for women's emancipation beginning in the twentieth century. Here, a formative cognitive process was brought to bear on the "deep waters of the person," on the "secret material structured by the unconscious." As a result of this process, we began to look upon the desiccated land of history with different eyes, which ultimately required the subversion of the existing order.[18]

It was with this presupposition that feminism attempted, at that time, to construct its own political lexicon, redefining words such as "democracy," "equality," "freedom," "organization," among others. Beginning from an analysis of the *self* in the context of the practice of consciousness-raising, feminism introduced new terms and concepts that arose from its radical theorization.[19] Feminist culture in the 1970s presented an exceptional balance between knowing, understood as a *formative* process (that incorporated fidelity to the body's memory, the sexual imaginary, and the particular experience of each individual), and a *transformative* impulse in the world. The latter was manifested in battles over divorce, abortion, family rights, and sexual violence. The mobilization of rights and liberatory practices were interwoven with one another; both aimed at broader discussions around sexuality and the dominance of male culture rather than separate pieces of legislative reform.

This emerging form of knowing, based on examination of the self, was localized on the conflictual border between the public and private spheres; it was a form of knowing that highlighted the body, sexuality, psychological and physical health, and it attended to the impact of a male-dominated society on these aspects of women's lives. The challenge it launched threatened established institutions, which not only obstructed women's efforts, but, in some cases, even held them hostage. It was a form of knowing that, as Rossana Rossanda understood, constituted "a true critique, and, therefore, a unilateral and antagonistic negation of the culture of the other."[20]

This new kind of knowing presented difficulties with respect to confronting entrenched historical constructions because of the radical nature of its initial assumption: the anomalous and unexpected female political subject for whom subjectivity was uniquely singular but also grounded in the collective. This subjectivity, enacted as a "speaking for oneself," did not merely denounce social disadvantages and discrimination. Rather, it was a subjectivity that arose in response to the *expropriation of women's very existence*, an expropriation that originated from the determination of female destiny as rooted in female sexuality (that is, procreation) and thus restricted women to the "natural" role of motherhood, a life of self-sacrifice, and an uncritical dedication to men. This new political subject was an affirmation of female liberty, which was understood as a slow process of liberation from the many internalized unfreedoms that women lived in the experience of love, in family and work relations, in sickness, in madness, and in the inurement of daily violence. With consciousness-raising, the focus of the cognitive process was shifted toward the body and memory; an approach that began with an examination of oneself was opposed to the generalizations of politics.

Reflecting on the birth of subjectivity and the experience of self-discovery, Carla Lonzi noted that the blocks and obstacles necessarily encountered in the process of consciousness-raising could and must be overcome in order for one's true individuality to emerge.[21]

But this process, which focused attention on the individual, required not only consideration of lived experience but the physical presence of others. Separatism offered women the opportunity to relate to one another *outside* of the male gaze. Female subjectivity was born from this particular relation of similarity. Consciousness-raising, however, was not the short-term strategy of a finite historical moment, as the Libreria delle donne di Milano [The Women's Bookstore of Milan] pointed out in its reconstruction of those years.[22] Theoretically, female subjectivity encompassed discourse on the body, sexuality, and, no less important, psychoanalysis. The enduring quality of this discourse is related to the fact that sexuality does not belong to this or that epoch; not only is it part of each individual's personal life, it is a significant structural element of society.

Manuela Fraire was absolutely correct when she wrote that consciousness-raising "was an instrument that was abandoned too early,"[23] and that its ripe fruits were, in part, harvested by certain writings that conserved its traces.[24]

Feminism encountered problems "when it extended itself beyond consciousness-raising groups and other small collectives in order to gain admission to the institutional domains of culture and politics, when it shifted from a movement to become more widespread. If the expansion was auspicious, it nevertheless posed risks: Not surprisingly, established cultural and political institutions expropriated and redefined the legacy produced by women."[25]

In the Modena conference on Feminist Studies in Italy (Studi femministi in Italia) in 1987, a split became apparent: One group wanted to protect "spaces of autonomy and self-management within the university, thereby activating moments of self-reflection on women's presence there as well as creating new paradigms for studying and learning." They wanted to "deconstruct and transform the various disciplines by introducing new and foreign forms of knowledge to them." In other words, they wanted to establish genuine and meaningful connections between the university and society. The second group wanted to focus on the creation of the female subject, to establish a "tradition" of women's authority and language. They argued that women needed a unique "symbolic order" upon which the female subject could be grounded. In the construction of a female identity able to participate in public life, the body ceased to be central, and the importance of the self and personal experience was sidelined. The notion of "female difference" put forward at the conference bore the signs of a reassuringly essentialist position—a position that became popular precisely because it seemed to bypass the slow, exacting nature of liberatory practices.[26]

In response to these positions, the journal *Lapis* took a different approach. Critical of both the notion of "difference" and the proliferation of "gender studies" in the academy, *Lapis*'s editorial team wanted to continue and develop the practices out of which feminism had grown: examination of the connections between politics and life, between self-knowledge and the other forms of discourse that we had imbibed. They sought a self-awareness capable of interrogating traditional forms of knowledge and the established powers of public life, and they called for a "geography rather than a genealogy," a kind of knowing able and willing to enter "disturbing landscapes" and unafraid to plumb male-female relations in all of their complexity and contradictions.

The political culture of women, which focused its attention on the body, personal history, and the relation between the individual and society, today plays the important role of asking questions pertinent to the contemporary context. The way in which it poses these questions avoids the simplification and erasure implicit in the use of terms such as "barbarism," "irrationality," and "regression." Feminism must not restrict itself to "female questions" (that is, issues of women's marginalization and equal representation, or social and family policies, etc.); indeed, it has much to offer, not only about specific issues such as artificial insemination, community centers, and male violence against women, but about matters that affect all of society, including the crises of political parties, the triumph of antipolitics, populism, the politics of security and risk, xenophobia, the crisis of the family, civil rights, and biotechnology.

On one hand, we need to return to the radical *point of view* that characterized feminism from the start—the perspective that saw the originary structure of all dualisms in the relation between the sexes. On the other hand, we must respond to the fact that the problems of the body and all that was previously considered to be "nonpolitical" now occupy center stage in the public domain, despite their misrepresentation as "ethically sensitive questions" and "problems of conscience"—labels intended to obscure their inherently political nature.

Unfortunately, these problems are framed very differently from the way in which we would frame them. They constitute the most significant matters of lived experience, but we no longer recount or live them. Interconnected, many of these problems are obscured by the powers and language of the public sphere.

In the 1970s, we discovered and explored connections between seemingly opposed poles. Today, we are confronted with an amalgam in which private and public, home and city, business and state seem to be devouring themselves. Public discourse increasingly dominates all discourse: instead of discussions about motherhood or abortion, we hear about "Law 40" or "Law 194." In other respects, personal life and relations prevail: public institutions are preoccupied with the prosaic and mundane, the minutiae of daily life, and public discourse is reduced to "common sense."

In order to undo this dangerous collapse of private and public, which feeds a growing populism, we need, once again, to examine and interrogate lived experience, and we must understand the ways in which our experience is bound to forms of knowledge and the power of institutions. In order to reappropriate and fully inhabit our own experience, we need *self*-knowledge, for only self-knowledge can provide the foundation for the kinds of knowledge produced by the culture of women. In other words, we need to learn what Laura Kreyder, the editor of *Lapis*, called a "salvific bilingualism": "Reasoning with our deep memory, the intimate language of infancy, and, simultaneously, with words, the language of social life, work, and institutions."[27] And we must learn how to negotiate the conflict that this *new knowledge* will bring forth.

Notes

Preface

1. [Confindustria is the acronym for the Confederazione generale dell'industria italiana (The General Confederation of Italian Industry). It is an association of the Italian employers' federation and the national Chamber of Commerce. It consists of some 113, 000 member companies and 4.2 million individuals.—Trans.]

2. Pierre Bourdieu, *Masculine Domination*, trans. Richard Nice (Palo Alto: Stanford University Press, 2002), 109.

Chapter One. The Body and the Polis

1. Otto Weininger, *Sex and Character: An Investigation of Fundamental Principles*, trans. L. Löb (Bloomington: Indiana University Press, 2005).

2. Giorgio Agamben, *Homo Sacer: Sovereign Power and Bare Life* (Torino: Einaudi, 1995), 10–11.

3. Jean-Luc Nancy, *Corpus* (Napoli: Cronopio, 1995), 56.

4. Sigmund Freud, *Civilization and Its Discontents*, trans. James Strachey (New York: W.W. Norton, 1961), 60–61.

5. Karl Marx, "Estranged Labour," in *The Economic and Philosophical Manuscripts of 1844*, at: https://www.marxists.org/archive/marx/works/1844/manuscripts/labour.htm.

6. Franco Rella, *Asterischi* (Milano: Feltrinelli, 1989), 83. See also his *Egli* (Mantova: Tre Lune, 1999), 100.

7. Jean-Luc Nancy, *Corpus*, trans. A. Moscati (Napoli: Cronopio, 2004), 89.

8. Ibid., 11.

9. Elvio Fachinelli, *Il bambino dalle uova d'oro* (Milano: Feltrinelli, 1974), 27.

10. Miguel Benasayag, *Contro il niente. Abc dell'impegno* (Milano: Feltrinelli, 2005), 47–49.

11. Roberto Andreotti and Federico De Melis, "Le elezioni di Agamben," *Il manifesto* 17 (March 2008).

12. Rossana Rossanda, *Le altre. Conversazioni sulle parole della politica* (Milano: Feltrinelli, 1989).

13. Rossanda, *Le altre*, 59–60.

14. Roberto Esposito, *Bios* (Torino: Einaudi, 2004).

15. Elvio Fachinelli, Luisa Muraro, and Giuseppe Sartori, eds., *L'erba Voglio. Practica non autoritaria nella Scuola* (Torino: Einaudi, 1971), 29–31.

16. Manuela Fraire and Rossana Rossanda, *La perdita*, ed. Lea Melandri (Torino: Bollati Boringhieri, 2008), 10–11.

17. Rossanda, *Le altre*, 86.

18. Luciana Percovich, *La coscienza nel corpo. Donne, salute e medicine negli anni settanta* (Milano: Fondazione Badaracco-Angeli, 2005), 62.

19. Lea Melandri, *Una visceralità indicibile. La pratica dell'inconscio nel movimento delle donne degli anni settanta* (Milano: Fondazione Bedaracco-Angeli, 2000), 198.

20. Manuela Fraire, ed., *Lessico politico delle donne. Donne e medicine* (Milano: Gulliver, 1978), 15–16.

21. *Liberazione*, 22, May 2008.

22. Agnese Seranis, *Smarrirsi in pensieri lunari* (Napoli: Graus, 2007), 93–94.

23. Agamben, *Homo Sacer*, 137.

24. Alessandra Facchi, "Il pensiero femminista sul diritto. Un percorso da Carol Gilligan a Tove Stang Dahl," in *Filosofi del diritto contemporaneo*, ed. Gianfrancesco Zanetti (Milano: Cortina, 1999), 133.

25. Libreria delle donne di Milano, *Non credere di avere dei diritti. La generazione delle libertà femminile nell'idea e nelle vicende di un gruppo di donne* (Torino: Rosenberg and Sellier, 1987).

26. Edoardo Boncinelli and Galeazzo Sciaretta, *Verso l'immortalità* (Milano: Cortina, 2005).

27. Günther Anders, *L'uomo è antiquate* (Torino: Bollati Boringhieri, 2003).

28. Jean-Luc Nancy, *L'intruso* (Napoli: Cronopio, 2000), 28–35.

29. Franco Rella, *Dall'esilio. La creazione artistica come testimonianza* (Milano: Feltrinelli, 2004), 112.

30. Sigmund Freud, *The Future of an Illusion*, trans. James Strachey (New York: W.W. Norton, 1989).

31. Cited in Fabrizio Ravelli, "L'officina dei buoni figli," *La Repubblica*, December 5, 2004.

32. Alexis de Tocqueville, *Democracy in America*, trans. Henry Reeve, released as an e-book in 2006, book 4, chapter 6, at: http://www.gutenberg.org/files/816/816-h/816-h.htm#link2HCH0073.

33. "Tutte storie," September/November 1999, 21.

34. Tiqqun, *Elementi per una teoria della Jeune Fille* (Torino: Bollati Boringhieri, 2003), 32.

35. "Declaration of Veronica Lario, Wife of Silvio Berlusconi," to ANSA, April 28, 2009.

36. Pierangiolo Berrettoni, *Il maschio al bivio* (Torino: Bollati Boringhieri, 2007), 17–18.

37. Alberto Asor Rosa, *L'ultimo paradosso* (Torino: Einaudi, 1986), 86.

Chapter Two. Loving Mothers

1. Paolo Mantegazza, *Le estasi umane* (Milano: Mantegazza, 1887), 158.

2. Alberto Asor Rosa, *L'ultimo paradosso* (Torino: Einaudi, 1986), 149.

3. Pierre Bourdieu, *Il dominio maschile*, trans. Alessandro Serra (Milano: Feltrinelli, 1998), 126.

4. Sigmund Freud, *Civilization and Its Discontents*, trans. James Strachey (New York: W.W. Norton, 1961), 13.

5. Elvio Fachinelli, *Il bambino dalle uova d'oro* (Milano: Feltrinelli, 1974), 234.

6. Freud, *Civilization and Its Discontents*, 23.

7. Ibid., 27.

8. Ibid., 29.

9. Ibid., 39.

10. Ibid., 44.

11. Ibid., 46–47.

12. Ibid., 48.

13. Ibid., 49–50.

14. Ibid., 50–52.

15. Ibid., 55.

16. Sigmund Freud, *Introduzione al narcisismo* (Torino: Boringhieri, 1976), 37, 54–55, 57.

17. Sigmund Freud, "Il perturbante," in *Opere*, vol. 9 (Torino: Boringhieri, 1977), 106.

18. Freud, *Civilization and Its Discontents*, 60.

19. James Hillman, *Un terribile amore per la guerra* (Milano: Adelphi, 2004), 186.

20. Sigmund Freud, "Carteggio con Einstein," in *Opere*, vol. 11 (Torino: Boringhieri, 1979), 298.

21. Paolo Mantegazza, *Fisiologia delle donne* (Milano: Brigola, 1879), 149.

22. Virginia Woolf, "Una stanza tutta per sé," in *Per le strade di Londra* (Milano: Garzanti, 1974), 300.

23. Workerism: A Marxian-inspired social and political movement that saw work as the principal structure of society, which needed to be firmly rooted in the hands of workers rather than in those who own the means of production. *Operaismo* is very aware of the impact of technology on the changing nature of work, and of the worker, through its power of abstraction.

24. Paolo Tabet, *La grande beffa. Sessualità delle donne e scambio sessuo-economico* (Rubettino: Soveria Mannelli, 2005).

25. Alexis de Tocqueville, *Democracy in America*, trans. Henry Reeve, released as e-book in 2006, book 4, chapter 6, at: http://www.gutenberg.org/files/816/816-h/816-h.htm#link2HCH0073.

26. Fachinelli, *Il bambino dalle uova d'oro*, 107–13.

27. Virginia Woolf, "Pensieri di pace durante un'incursione aerea," in Ead., *Per le strade di Londra*, 148–52.

28. Jean-Jacques Rousseau, "Sophie or Woman," in *Émile*, book 5, trans. Barbara Foxley, www.gutenberg.org/cache/epub/5427/pg5427-images.html. Accessed July 28, 2015.

29. "Il lavoro domestico e di cura non pagato: Una sfida politica e teorica sempre più attuale" Antonella Picchio, Seminar held at the Libera Università delle Donne, March 27, 2010, www.universitadelledonne.it.

30. Lea Melandri, *Sibilla Aleramo. Un pudore selvaggio, una selvaggia nudità*, in Ead., *Come nasce il sogno d'amore* (Torino: Bollati Boringhieri, 2002), 27.

31. Ibid., 104.

32. Luisa Pogliana, *Donne senza guscio. Percorsi femminili in azienda* (Milano: Guerini, 2008).

33. "Divenire-donna della politica." Excerpt from the journal *Posse* (Rome: Manifestolibri, 2003), 54.

34. Pogliana, *Donna senza guscio*, 104–05.

35. Ibid., 121–28.

36. Elisabeth Badinter, *Le conflit: La femme et la mère* (Paris: Flammarion, 2010).

37. In *La Repubblica delle donne*, n. 681, February 13, 2010.

38. Paola Leonardi and Ferdinanda Vigliani, *Perché non abbiamo avuto figli. Donne 'speciali' si raccontano* (Milano: Angeli, 2009).

39. [Published in English as Sibilla Aleramo, *A Woman*, trans. Rosalind Delmar (Oakland: University of California Press.—Trans.]

40. Sibilla Aleramo, *Una donna* (Milano: Feltrinelli, 1980), 74–180.

41. Mantegazza, *Le estasi umane*, 156–57.

42. Carla Lonzi, *Sputiamo su Hegel. La donna clitoridea e la donna vaginale e altri scritti* (Milano: Scritti di Rivolta Femminile, 1974), 139–40.

43. Gruppo lavoro della Libreria delle donne di Milano, *Immagina che il lavoro* (Milano: 2009).

44. Eleonora Cirant, "I racconti del corpo" (unpublished).

Chapter Three. The Circle of Men

1. Alberto Asor Rosa, *L'ultimo paradosso* (Torino: Einaudi, 1986), 79–80.

2. "Maschi, perché uccidete le donne?," *Liberazione*, November 6–7, 2005.

3. Sigmund Freud, *Civilization and Its Discontents*, trans. James Strachey (New York: W.W. Norton, 1961), 58.

4. Virginia Woolf, *Three Guineas*, www.gutenberg.net.au/ebooks02/0200931.txt. Accessed August 7, 2015.

5. Pierre Bourdieu, *Il dominio maschile*, trans. Alessandro Serra (Milano: Feltrinelli, 1998), 136.

6. Carla Lonzi, *Sputiamo su Hegel* (Milano: Rivolta Femminile, 1974), 77.

7. Stefano Ciccone, *Essere maschi. Tra potere e libertà* (Torino: Rosenberg and Sellier, 2009), 59.

8. Johann Jakob Bachofen, *Il matriarcato* [*Matriarchy*], vol. 1 (Torino: Einaudi, 1988), 116.

9. Jules Michelet, *L'amore* (Milano: Rizzoli, 1987 [1858]),64, 95, 58, 106.

10. Sándor Ferenczi, *Thalassa* (Milano: Cortina, 1993), 39–43, 35, 36, 47.

11. Ibid., 58–67, 70.

12. Ibid., 46.

13. Carlo Michelstaedter, *Epistolario* (Milano: Adelphi, 1983), 341.

14. Luce Irigaray, *Elemental Passions*, trans. Joanne Collie and Judith Still (New York: Routledge, 1992). Each passage is followed by the page reference to the text.

15. Ciccone, *Essere maschi*, 21.

16. Benjamin Constant, *The Liberty of the Ancients Compared with That of the Moderns*, ed. Jonathan Bennett, nationallibertyalliance.org/files/docs/Books/Constant%20The%20Liberty%20of%20the%20Ancients%20Compared%20with%20that%20of%20the%20Moderns.pdf. Accessed August 11, 2015.

17. Fachinelli, *Il bambino dalle uova d'oro*, 171–76.

18. Rossana Rossanda, *Le altre. Conversazioni sulle parole della politica* (Milano: Feltrinelli, 1989), 87.

Chapter Four. The Disquieting Slumber of the West

1. Samuel P. Huntington, *Lo scontro delle civiltà*, trans. S. Minucci (Milano: Garganti, 2000). [Originally published in English as *The Clash of Civilizations and the Remaking of World Order* (New York: Simon and Schuster, 2007).—Trans.]

2. Elena Pulcini, *L'individuo senza passioni* (Torino: Bollati Boringhieri, 2001), 167.

3. Marc Augé, *Nonluoghi* (Milano: Elèuthera, 1993).

Notes to Chapter Five

4. Richard Sennett, *L'uomo flessibile. Le consequenze del nuovo capitalismo sulla vita personale*, trans. Mirko Tavosanis (Milano: Feltrinelli, 2001). [Originally published in English as *The Corrosion of Character: The Personal Consequences of work in the New Capitalism* (New York: W.W. Norton, 1998).]

5. Miguel Benasayag and Gérard Schmit, *L'epoca delle passioni tristi* (Milano: Feltrinelli, 2004).

6. Zygmunt Bauman, *Liquid Modernity* (London: Polity, 2000).

7. Sennett, *L'uomo flessibile*.

8. Fachinelli, *Il bambino dalle uova d'oro*, 27.

9. Miguel Benasayag and Angélique Del Rey, *Elogio del conflitto* (Milano: Feltrinelli, 2008), 203.

10. "Neither Lenin nor Trotsky Can Help Us," *Liberazione*, July 2008.

11. Benasayag and Del Rey, *Elogio del conflitto*, 9.

12. Ulrich Beck, "Le vite smarrite nella società del rischio," *La Repubblica*, June 7, 2008.

13. Guido Viale, "Rifiuti urbani e rifiuti umani," *La Repubblica*, May 23, 2008.

14. Benasayag and Del Rey, *Elogio del conflitto*, 197.

15. Benasayag and Del Rey, *Elogio del conflitto*, 187.

Chapter Five. The Unstoppable Revolution

1. Elvio Fachinelli, *Il bambino dalle uova d'oro* (Milano: Feltrinelli, 1974), 141.

2. *Liberazione*, May 28, 2008.

3. A factory located in Forlì that produced various appliances.

4. "Lo Chopin partiva. Storie di donne," *Una Città*, Forlì (2007): 227.

5. Quotation appears in Lea Melandri, ed., *L'erba voglio (1971–1977)*, in *Il desiderio dissidente* (Milano: Baldini and Castoldi, 1988), 120–21, 45.

6. Fachinelli, *Il bambino dalle uova d'oro*, 212–47.

7. Ibid., 139.

8. Rossana Rossanda, *Le altre. Conversazione sulle parole della politica* (Milano: Feltrinelli, 1989), 211.

9. Fachinelli, *Il bambino dalle uova d'oro*, 20.

10. Elvio Fachinelli, Luisa Muraro, Vaiani Sartori, and Giuseppe Sartori, eds., *L'erba voglio: pratica non autoritaria nella scuola* (Torino: Einaudi, 1971).

11. Fachinelli, *Il bambino dalle uova d'oro*, 25.

12. Ibid., 44.

13. Fachinelli, Muraro, Sartori, and Sartori, *L'erba voglio*, 272.

14. Melandri, *L'erba voglio*, 163–64.

15. Luisa Muraro, "Le donne invisibili," in *L'erba voglio*, ed. Lea Melandri, 244–45.

16. *I movimenti femministi*, in *Italia*, ed. Rosalba Spagnoletti (Milano: Savelli, 1977), 57–58.

17. *Sottosopra. Esperienze dei gruppi femministi in Italia*, Gruppo del giornale, Milano, 1973.

18. Rossanda, *Le altre*.

19. Manuela Fraire, ed., *Lessico politico delle donne. Donne e medicine* (Milano: Gulliver, 1978).

20. Rossanda, *Le altre*, 211.

21. Carla Lonzi, *Sputiamo su Hegel. La donna clitoridea e la donna vaginale e altri scritti* (Milano: Scritti di Rivolta Femminile, 1974).

22. Libreria delle donne di Milano, *Non credere di avere dei diritti. La generazione delle libertà femminile nell'idea e nelle vicende di un gruppo di donne* (Torino: Rosenberg and Sellier, 1987).

23. Fraire, *Lessico politico delle donne*, 186.

24. Fraire refers in particular to the Milanese group Sexuality and Writing, which published *A Zig Zag* in 1978, and to *Lapis: Percorsi della riflessione femminile*, a volume of the journal that explored the experiences of the women in the Associazione per una Libera Università di Milano. See *Lapis. Sezione aurea di una rivista, 1978–1997* (Roma: manifestolibri, 1998).

25. *Atti del seminario internazionale "Centri di ricerca e documentazione delle donne. Esperienze di organizzazione e metodi di archiviazione"* (Milan: Centro di studi storici sul movimento di liberazione della donne in Italia, 1981), 4.

26. Anna Rossi Doria and Maria Cristina Marcuzzo, eds., *La ricerca delle donne. Studi femministi in Italia* (Torino: Rosenberg and Sellier, 1987).

27. *Lapis*, 10.

Index

1968: Elvio Facchinelli's articles of, 116–118; feminism in, 122; lessons of, 128; movements of, 112; and new way of being and living, 109; Rudi Dutschke's interview in, 121–122, 128; shifting borders between the body and the polis, 58; student movement, 8, 116, 117, 119, 122, 124; summer of, 113; University of Milan in, 15, 119

abortion: campaign against, 10, 20, 21; decriminalization of, 20–21; divergent views on, 19–20; and female self-determination, 21; and feminism, 16, 22, 126, 132; group A/Matrix Roma on, 20–21; legalization of, 70; political Left on, 13, 19; and public discourse, 135; and the question of law and rights, 19–21; and secularism, 20; and sexuality, 19–21
Afghanistan, 97
Agamben, Giorgio, 3–4, 11, 22–23
aggression, 4–5, 8, 41, 49–50, 51, 59, 77–78, 102, 103–104
Aleramo, Sibilla, 38, 61–62, 130; *Una donna*, 69
Alfa Romeo, 115

alienation, 3, 5–6, 9, 17–18, 93, 124
Le altre (Rossanda), 17–18
Anders, Günther, 24
antipolitical attitudes, 9, 11, 13, 16–17, 114, 129–130, 134
L'Asilo di Porta Ticinese (Milan), 15, 92, 119
Asor Rosa, Alberto, 35, 38; *L'ultimo paradosso*, 73–74

Bachofen, Johann Jakob, 69, 83–84, 85
Badinter, Elisabeth, 70–71; *Le conflit: La femme et la mère*, 68
Baudelaire, Charles, 28
Bauman, Zygmunt, 101
Beck, Ulrich, 106–107
Benasayag, Miguel, 9, 100, 109; *Elogio del conflitto*, 105–106, 107–108
Benedict XVI, Pope, 10
Berlusconi, Silvio, 34, 35, 36, 57, 93
"Berlusconism," 59
Berrettoni, Pierangiolo, 35
biopolitics, 94, 114; affirmative, 15, 129; definition, 15; powers of, 8
biopower, 8, 127
biotechnology, 23–24, 55, 127, 135
Bloch, Ernst, 115
body: as bare, 7; and biopower, 127;

body (*cont'd*)
and church, 55; commodification of, 7, 57; in contrast to an I, 17, 25; and difference, 26–27; erotic view of, 62; exploitation of, 33; expropriation of, 18; feeling, 28; as forced labor, 6–7; fragility of, 103; and law, 16–23; male domination of, 4; manipulability and transformational capacity of, 31–32; and medicine, 55; and modern democracy, 22–23; mortality of, 8, 98; as nature, 4, 31; as object of rights, 16, 17; objectification of, 55–56, 80; in opposition to thought, 4, 12–13, 26, 38, 63, 80, 114, 128, 131; and oppression, 75; and polis, 4, 7–8, 36, 58, 125, 127; political nature of, 55, 135; primary view of women as, 66–67, 80, 124, 125, 130; as prison or tomb of the soul, 4; as property, 16, 17; in the public and in the private sphere, 16; reappropriation of, 18, 21, 125; reductionist view of, 4; and religion, 16, 33; return to, 9, 15, 106, 119, 125, 126, 128, 129, 132; separated from human activity, 5; and sexuality, 4, 124; and state, 55; and suffering, 41; thinking, 9, 14, 16; and the uncanny, 48–49
body politic, 16
body-world, 40
Bourdieu, Pierre, 38; *Masculine Domination*, 81

capital: and labor, 81; surplus, 7
capitalism, 15, 102, 106, 124
Catholicism: battle against abortion, 20; fundamentalist, 10, 13; invasion of the political domain, 12; *see also* church; religion

Cecchi, Emilio, 62
Center for the Health of Women (Padova), 18
church: and body, 55; family and, 76; powers of, 8, 11; and social transformation, 121; and state, 12; supporting biopower, 8, 127; *see also* Catholicism; religion
Ciccone, Stefano, 89; *Essere maschi*, 83
Cirant, Eleonora, 71
Circolo De Amicis (Milan), 19
Una Città (journal), 115
civilization: and ancient dichotomies, 26; coercion of work and, 5; in contrast to barbarism, 98, 103; in contrast to human drives, 3; discontent of, 37–38; and eros, 44, 46–47; incompatibility with happiness, 42; love and, 5, 44–47; and male "superiority," 35–36; parents of, 44; regulation of reciprocal relationships, 43; and religion, 10; and sexuality, 46; "vexatious factor," 51; work of, 45
Civilization and Its Discontents (Freud), 4–5, 39–47, 49–50, 77–78
civilizations, "clash of," 94, 96
commodification of: desire, 33; female body, 57; labor and the worker, 6, 7; women, 80
communism, 4–5, 8, 121
Le conflit: La femme et la mère (Badinter), 68
Constant, Benjamin, *The Liberty of the Ancients Compared with That of the Moderns*, 90
consumerism, 32, 93, 107, 113, 118, 127
Croce, Benedetto, 62

Darwinism, Social, 29

Del Rey, Angélique, *Elogio del conflitto*, 105–106, 107–108
Demau (Milan), 124
democracy: Alexis de Tocqueville on, 30, 58; "aporia" of modern, 22–23; and body, 22–23; direct, 121–122; "governability" replacing, 128; as *oikonomia*, 11; and political Left, 14; redefining, 131; and totalitarianism, 91; and women, 52, 130
Democracy in America (Tocqueville), 58
"Il desiderio dissidente" (Fachinelli), 116
despotism, 30–31
dichotomies, 16, 26, 51, 67, 90
Una donna (Aleramo), 69
La donna clitoridea e la donna vaginale (Lonzi) *see Sputiamo su Hegel: La donna clitoridea e la donna vaginale* (Lonzi)
Donna senza guscio: Precorsi femminili in azienda (Pogliana), 63–68
Dutschke, Rudi, 121–122, 128

Economic and Philosophic Manuscripts of 1844 (Marx), 3, 5–6
economization, 9, 113–114
Einstein, Albert, correspondence with Sigmund Freud, 51
Elogio del conflitto (Benasayag & Del Rey), 105–106, 107–108
emancipation, 33, 131; and body, 9, 75; configured as flight from devalued feminity, 53; and equal rights, 80; and family, 53; male model of, 67; questionable, 59; and separatism, 124–125; and sexuality, 75
Émile (Rousseau), 60–61, 88
enigma of: dualism, 3; history, 3; origins, 80; sex, 3, 91; war, 91

Enlightenment, 12
equality, 8, 14; advance of, 56; Alexis de Tocqueville on, 30–31; and difference, 23, 67, 70, 93; fragility of, 91; redefining, 131; "relations of," 120
L'erba voglio (book), 119–120, 121
L'erba voglio (journal), 112, 116, 119, 122–124, 126
eros: and civilization, 44, 46–47; "disturbing" element, 48; dream of, 7; essence of, 82; historical cunning of, 8, 103; and thanatos, 48–51, 77
Esposito, Roberto, 15
Essere maschi (Ciccone), 83
ethics: and politics, 10–16; "public," 13, 17; religious, 13; "secular," 13
eugenics, 29
European Union, 97
euthanasia, 13

Facchi, Alessandra, 23
Fachinelli, Elvio, 8, 40, 59, 92, 103–104, 113, 118, 119; "Il desiderio dissidente," 116; "Gruppo chiuso o gruppo aperto?," 116; "Masse a tre anni," 119; "Il paradosso della ripetizione," 116–117
family: and church, 76; combining work and, 64, 65; in conflict with larger community, 45; and domestic violence, 54–55; dream of harmonious, 68; exalted as refuge and security, 54; in feminism, 16, 125, 126, 127, 132, 134; as first building block of social life, 98; in the Italian constitution, 6; and love, 44; metaphor of, 51; new freedoms around, 36; opposing male and female roles, 6; political Left on, 128; prolonging infancy, 78;

family (*cont'd*)
rights, 16; as sacred, 11; and state, 53; two pairs of, 43; women and, 45, 53, 62, 65, 80; as "workshop of good children," 29

female body, 9, 11, 24, 36; and biopower, 127; commodification of, 57; debasing of, 88; as deprived of an I, 17; as erotic body, 56; as first "other," 128; as male projection, 22, 60, 75; male's appropriation of, 49–51, 83; as maternal body, 56; persecution by men, 78–79; questionable emancipation, 59; and role of mother, 78–79, 82, 85–87, 97; as viewed by the public, 39; violability of, 52–53

feminism: in 1968, 122; in the 1970s, 126, 131–132; and abortion, 16, 22, 126, 132; antiauthoritarian and liberatory, 126; and the "aporia" of modern democracy, 22–23; attitude towards the law, 23; awareness produced by, 54; and body, 9, 21, 125, 135; on "body politic," 16–17; Carla Lonzi's radical, 69–70; contributions of, 14, 114, 129; current revival of, 57; decriminalization of abortion, 20–21; dreams of, 56; and dualism, 80, 126, 135; enduring lessons, 21; and the equality/difference binary, 67, 70; extreme protest of, 118; family in, 16, 125, 126, 127, 132, 134; female "difference," 21–22; and "feminization of work," 64; first groups in Italy, 124; indifferent or hostile responses to, 55; and liberation, 9; on liberty, 14, 17–18; in Milan, 112; narrative account of oneself, 18; and nonauthoritarian movements, 127, 129; and the power of the word, 127; and questionable form of emancipation, 59; rethinking freedom, 93–94; self-consciousness and conscious-raising, 126, 131–132, 133, 134; and sexuality, 91; transforming essential human experiences misrepresented as "unchangeable," 91–92; universal, 130; "valorization of differences," 63; *see also* women's movement

feminist revolution, 17, 55, 80, 91–92, 94, 118, 124, 129, 131

Feminist Studies in Italy, conference in Modena, 133–134

Ferenczi, Sándor, *Thalassa*, 85–87

Forlì, 115

Fraire, Manuela, 17, 133

freedom: and aporia of democracy, 23; "to be," 14; constitution of, 11; and dependency, 100, 103; exchange for safety, 91; and fear of anonymity, 97; male, and dependency on mother, 88; as male "natural" privilege, 76, 77; and necessity, 13, 61–62; negative sense of, 89, 91; Paola Redaelli on, 93–94; paradox of, 29–30; patriarchical, 91; and politics, 90; power to give birth as gesture of, 71; in the public sense of personhood, 89; restrictions to women's personal, 21; rethought by feminism, 93–94, 131; and servitude, 31; of western women, 10; of women, as threat to men, 54; *see also* liberation; liberty

Freud, Sigmund, 3, 10, 39, 51, 82, 87, 98, 100; *Civilization and Its Discontents*, 4–5, 39–47, 49–50, 77–78; correspondence with Albert Einstein, 51; *The Future of an Illusion*, 28, 41;

On Narcissism: An Introduction,
47–48; "The Uncanny," 48–49;
The Unhappiness of Society, 39
The Future of an Illusion (Freud), 28, 41

Gentilizi, Tiziana, 115
group A/Matrix Roma, 20–21
"Gruppo chiuso o gruppo aperto?"
  (Fachinelli), 116

Habeas Corpus Act (1679), 22
health: children's, 60; and exploitation of the body, 33; mask of perfect, 101; obsession with, 24; and politics, 127, 129; psychological and physical, 132; and reappropriation of the body, 125; right to, 18; and self-determination, 21; and sickness, 26, 103; women's, 126; *see also* medicine
Hillman, James, 50
historical materialism, 12
"Hitlerism," 59
homophobia, 128
homosexuality, 19, 81, 115, 126
Huntington, Samuel P., 96

individualism, 30, 31, 32, 90, 101, 106, 114, 115
Ingrao, Pietro, 14–15
inseminiation, artificial, 13, 24, 134
Iraq, 97
Irigaray, Luce, 88–89
Islam, fundamentalist, 10
Islamic veil, 96

Kreyder, Laura, 135

labor: and capital, 81; collective, 22, 120; commodification of, 6, 7; domestic, 18, 80–81, 126; exploitation of, 15, 123; extra, performed by women, 68; and female nature, 64–65; forced, 5–6, 7; organization of, 14–15, 64; sexual division of, 53, 63, 90, 128, 129; *see also* work
Lapis: Percorsi della riflessione femminile (journal), 112, 134
Lario, Veronica, 34, 57
law, and body, 16–23
Left, political: and abortion, 13, 19; centrality of work, 55, 114; and the current political crisis, 11–12; defeat of, 113; on democracy, liberty, equality, 14; division of, 115–116; on family, 128; inability to renewal, 128–129; and *operaismo*, 55; original sin of individualism, 106; and the question of life, 15; and rise of Catholic fundamentalism, 13; and separatism, 124–125; and subjective needs, 113; and women's personal freedom, 21
Leonardi, Paola, *Perché non abbiamo avuto figli*, 68
lesbianism, 21, 81, 115
Lessico politico delle donne: Donne e medicine, 19–20
liberation: in contrast to liberty, 125; feminism and, 9; forms of dualism, 67; as "freedom from," 91; slow process of, 132; struggle for, 22; student movement's focus on, 116; women's, 14–15; *see also* freedom
Liberazione (newspaper), 73–74, 105, 113
liberty: Benjamin Constant on, 90; broadening of female, 89, 132; "children of," 29; in contrast to liberation, 125; and female identity, 17–18; as "freedom to be," 14; and necessity, 13, 16; *see also* freedom

The Liberty of the Ancients Compared with That of the Moderns (Constant), 90
Libreria delle donne di Milano, 133
life, questions of, 11, 12, 13, 15, 27
Lonzi, Carla, 133; *Sputiamo su Hegel: La donna clitoridea e la donna vaginale*, 69–70, 81–82
Lotta Femminista, 80

male body: debasing of, 88; role in the reproductive process, 83
Manifesto (newspaper), 11
Mantegazza, Paolo, 37, 53, 69
Marx, Karl, 12, 114; *Economic and Philosophic Manuscripts of 1844*, 3, 5–6
Marxism, 116, 128
Marxists, 9, 80, 117, 118
Masculine Domination (Bourdieu), 81
"Masse a tre anni" (Fachinelli), 119
materialism, historical, 12
medicine: and body, 55; invasive practices of, 125; modern, 103; and power-subverting practices, 108; and the state, 18; and technology, 26; and women's health, 126; *see also* health
Melandri, Lea: *L'erba voglio* (journal), 112, 116, 119, 122–124, 126; interview with *La Repubblica delle Donne*, 68; *Lapis: Percorsi della riflessione femminile* (journal), 112, 134; on Milan, 111–113
men: Alberto Asor Rosa on, 73–74; Stefano Ciccone on, 83, 89
Michelet, Jules, 69, 83, 84–85, 87
Michelstaedter, Carlo, 87
Milan, 122–123; Alfa Romeo, 115; L'Asilo di Porta Ticinese, 15, 92, 119; Circolo De Amicis, 19; Demau, 124; Lea Melandri on, 111–113; Libreria delle donne di Milano, 133; solitary death in, 98; University of Milan, 15, 119; Via Cherubini collective, 126–127
military, 76, 124
misogyny, 114, 128
Modena, conference on Feminist Studies in Italy, 133–134
Montessori, Maria, 80
mother-child relation, 5, 27, 37, 39, 40, 43, 47–49, 78, 81–89, 94
mother-homeland, 50
motherhood: different attitudes towards, 71; and exploitation of women, 62; and female body, 78–79, 82, 85–87, 97; and "female competencies," 63; female restriction to, 51, 60, 79, 125, 132; as foundation of female identity, 70; and love, 63, 68; and necessity, 70; and professional career, 56, 65, 68; public discourse on, 135; role of, 50; sacrifice in, 61; and seduction, 64; and sex, 77; and unpaid labor, 80–81
motherland, 50
Murard-Yovanovitch, Flore, 113–114
Muraro, Luisa, 123–124
murder, of women, 52, 55, 70, 78

Nancy, Jean-Luc, 4, 7, 9, 25–26
narcissism, 39, 41, 47–48, 100
On Narcissism: An Introduction (Freud), 47–48
necessity: and freedom, 13, 61–62; and liberty, 13, 16; in life and politics, 94; and love, 38; of men's "destiny," 75; and motherhood, 70; as parent of civilization, 44; and work, 41, 43–44, 115
New York, September 11, 2001 attacks, 101, 102
Non credere di avere dei diritti, 23
nonauthoritarian movements, 8,

13–14, 15, 91–92, 116, 119, 120, 121, 124, 127

operaismo, 55, 128, 140

Padova, Center for the Health of Women, 18
"Il paradosso della ripetizione" (Fachinelli), 116–117
"party," idea of, 14
patriarchy: endurance of, 76; and expropriation of female existence, 80; flexibility and adaptability of, 64; freedom as source of contradiction, 91; interests and well-being of men, 85; and nationalism, 50; as original alienation, 6, 9; in the private and public sphere, 63–64, 74; reinvigoration of, 127–128; and sexism, 52; vaginal woman as woman of, 70; and weakness of men, 61
Perché non abbiamo avuto figli (Leonardi & Vigliani), 68
La perdita (Rossanda), 17
Picchio, Antonella, 61
Pietropolli Charmet, Gustavo, 28
Plato's cave, 4
Pogliana, Luisa, *Donna senza guscio: Precorsi femminili in azienda*, 63–68
polis: birth of, 4, 53, 118; and body, 4, 7–8, 36, 58, 125, 127; disturbing ordered rituals of, 35; entering, 7–8, 125; exclusion from, 8, 89; and the individual, 89–90; and private home, 22, 118, 127
populism, 11, 129, 134, 135
property: body as, 16, 17; private, 4–5, 30, 49, 90, 124, 126
psychoanalysis, 3, 19, 80, 114, 118, 133
"public ethics," 13, 17

Quaderni piacentini (journal), 116, 121
questions of life, 11, 12, 13, 15, 27

racism, 114, 128
rape, 52, 54–55, 78
Redaelli, Paola, 93–94
religion: of ascetic warriors, 74; and body, 16, 33; and civilization, 10; dominion over women by, 27; fundamentalist, 10, 13, 28, 130; New Age, 10; and politics, 12; renewed interest in, 10, 96–97; and the secular, 13; Sigmund Freud on, 41; and techno-science, 25; traditional values of, 10; women's self-sacrifice as, 69; *see also* Catholicism; church
religious ethics, 13
Rella, Franco, 6–7, 28
La Repubblica delle Donne (journal), 68
Revelli, Marco, 105, 109
revolution: of 1968, 113, 116–117, 122; ascetic tradition of, 15; feminist, 17, 55, 80, 91–92, 94, 118, 124, 129, 131; Marxist idea of, 117; Marxist-Leninist parties, 8–9; socialist, 14
Right, political: antipolitics of, 114; and the current political crisis, 11–12; cynicism of, 129; original sin of individualism, 106; and subjective needs, 113; and women's personal freedom, 21
rights: and abortion, 19–21; for biological life, 27; body as object of, 16, 17; civil, 20, 135; family, 16; female workers knowledge of, 66; as fragile freedom, 91; and liberatory practices, 132; and the relations of production, 12; struggle for, 22, 56, 80, 115, 126; for the "unwanted," 103

Rolland, Romain, 39
Rossanda, Rossana, 1, 5, 14, 93, 118, 126, 132; *Le altre*, 17–18; *La perdita*, 17
Rousseau, Jean-Jacques, 130; *Émile*, 60–61, 88

schism, original, 3–4
Schmit, Gérard, 100
science, 8, 11, 13, 24, 25, 28, 31, 42, 103, 108, 125, 127
secular ethics, 13
secularism: and abortion, 20; change of, 12; concept of the private, 15; and religion, 10, 13
Sennett, Richard, 99, 101
September 11, 2001 attacks, New York, 101, 102
Seranis, Agnese, *Smarrirsi in pensiere lunari*, 22
sexism, 52, 75, 80, 128
sexuality: annihilation of female, 125; and body, 4, 124; and civilization, 46; conception of, 15; conflation with maternity, 80–81; "disturbing" element, 48; and dominance of male culture, 22, 132; and emancipation, 75; and feminism, 91; and the media, 58; in personal and public spheres, 34, 126, 133; as political matter, 127, 129; and politics, 33–34, 36; and question of abortion, 19–21; and questionable emancipation, 59; and relation between the sexes, 13; separation from procreation, 70; Sigmund Freud's reading of female, 87; violent aspect, 82; war on female, 52
Smarrirsi in pensiere lunari (Seranis), 22
solitude, 41, 65, 98, 99, 100, 112–113
Sottosopra (journal), 126–127

South Pacific, tsunami, 101, 102, 104
Sputiamo su Hegel: La donna clitoridea e la donna vaginale (Lonzi), 69–70, 81–82
state: and body, 55; and business, 135; and church, 12; expropriation of female bodies, 18, 20; and family, 53; powers of, 8, 11; and the private, 15; and security, 128; suffering caused by, 42; supporting biopower, 8, 127
stem cell research, 13
student movement of 1968, 8, 116, 117, 119, 122, 124

Tabet, Paolo, 57
technology: dominion over life, 24, 26; dominion over nature, 41; "fabulous" bodies of, 8; Godlike character of, 42; and human reproduction, 27–28; and medicine, 26; omnipotence of, 10; possibility of immortality, 23–24; of reanimation, 24; and science, 25; *see also* biotechnology
Thalassa (Ferenczi), 85–87
thanatos, 48–51, 77
thinking body, 9, 14, 16; and feeling body, 28
"Thoughts on Peace in an Air Raid" (Woolf), 59–60
Three Guineas (Woolf), 79
Ticinese, Porta, 15
Tiqqun, 33
Tocqueville, Alexis de, 30–31, 90, 114; *Democracy in America*, 58
tsunami, South Pacific, 101, 102, 104

L'ultimo paradosso (Asor Rosa), 73–74
"The Uncanny" (Freud), 48–49
The Unhappiness of Society (Freud) *see Civilization and Its Discontents* (Freud)

Università Bocconi, 56
University of Milan, 15, 119
utility, demand for, 97, 106, 108

Vatican *see* Catholicism
Via Cherubini collective (Milan), 126–127
Viale, Guido, 107
Vigliani, Fernanda, *Perché non abbiamo avuto figli*, 68

war, 11, 24, 32, 56, 102; enigma of, 91; on female sexuality, 52, 79; logic of, 50, 108; love for, 50; necessity of, 5; between the sexes, 50, 86–87; Sigmund Freud's correspondence with Albert Einstein on, 51
Weininger, Otto, 3
women's liberation, 14–15
women's movement: analysis of sexism in Italy, 80; connections between sexuality and politics, 33–34, 36; and economization, 9; grounding in the embodied self, 124; historians' reconstruction of, 22; impact of, 129; message of, 18; and politics of life, 129–130; relation between the sexes, 13; and unpaid labor by women, 80–81; *see also* feminism
Woolf, Virginia, 54; "Thoughts on Peace in an Air Raid," 59–60; *Three Guineas*, 79
work: assembly-line versus today's, 115–116; bodies and, 7, 18; centrality of, 55, 114; of civilization, 45; coercion of, 5, 43–44; combining family and, 64, 65; domestic, 125; "feminization" of, 11–12, 53, 57, 64, 127; "flexibility" of, 103; linked to necessity, 41, 43–44, 115; and love, 5, 43, 84, 100; primacy of, 114; society of, 113; women and, 14–15, 56, 62–64, 65–68, 80, 131; *see also* labor
worker, 33, 66, 70, 80, 92, 114, 115–116, 116, 120, 122, 124; alienation of, 6; commodification of, 6, 7; immigrant, 95
workerism *see operaismo*

xenophobia, 96, 114, 128, 134

Zanussi (Forlì), 115